PLAY ON SHAKESPEARE

Edward III

PLAY ON SHAKESPEARE

All's Well That Ends Well	Virginia Grise
Antony and Cleopatra	Christopher Chen
As You Like It	David Ivers
The Comedy of Errors	Christina Anderson
Coriolanus	Sean San José
Cymbeline	Andrea Thome
Edward III	Octavio Solis
Hamlet	Lisa Peterson
Henry IV	Yvette Nolan
Henry V	Lloyd Suh
Henry VI	Douglas P. Langworthy
Henry VIII	Caridad Svich
Julius Caesar	Shishir Kurup
King John	Brighde Mullins
King Lear	Marcus Gardley
Love's Labour's Lost	Josh Wilder
Macbeth	Migdalia Cruz
Measure for Measure	Aditi Brennan Kapil
The Merchant of Venice	Elise Thoron
The Merry Wives of Windsor	Dipika Guha
A Midsummer Night's Dream	Jeffrey Whitty
Much Ado About Nothing	Ranjit Bolt
Othello	Mfoniso Udofia
Pericles	Ellen McLaughlin
Richard II	Naomi Iizuka
Richard III	Migdalia Cruz
Romeo and Juliet	Hansol Jung
The Taming of the Shrew	Amy Freed
The Tempest	Kenneth Cavander
Timon of Athens	Kenneth Cavander
Titus Andronicus	Amy Freed
Troilus and Cressida	Lillian Groag
Twelfth Night	Alison Carey
The Two Gentlemen of Verona	Amelia Roper
The Two Noble Kinsmen	Tim Slover
The Winter's Tale	Tracy Young

Edward III

by
William Shakespeare

Modern verse translation by
Octavio Solis

Dramaturgy by
Kimberly Colburn

Arizona Center
for Medieval and
Renaissance Studies
ACMRS PRESS
Arizona State University
Tempe, Arizona
2022

Publication of Play On Shakespeare is assisted by
generous support from the Hitz Foundation.
For more information, please visit www.playonshakespeare.org

Published by ACMRS Press
Arizona Center for Medieval and Renaissance Studies,
Arizona State University, Tempe, Arizona
www.acmrspress.com

Library of Congress Cataloging-in-Publication Data
Names: Solis, Octavio, author. | Shakespeare, William, 1564-1616. |
    Colburn, Kimberly, contributor.
Title: Edward III / by William Shakespeare ; modern verse translation by
    Octavio Solis ; dramaturgy by Kimberly Colburn.
Other titles: Edward the Third | Edward III (Drama)
Description: Tempe, Arizona : ACMRS Press, 2022. | Series: Play on
    Shakespeare | Summary: "This translation of the play provides all
    of the complexity and richness of the original while renewing the
    allusions and metaphors lost through time"-- Provided by publisher.
Identifiers: LCCN 2022012397 (print) | LCCN 2022012398 (ebook) |
    ISBN 9780866987813 (paperback) | ISBN 9780866987820 (ebook)
Subjects: LCSH: Edward III, King of England, 1312-1377--Drama. |
    Great Britain--History--Edward III, 1327-1377--Drama. | LCGFT:
    Biographical drama. | Historical drama.
Classification: LCC PR2878.E39 S65 2022 (print) | LCC PR2878.E39
    (ebook) | DDC 822.3/3--dc23/eng/20220317
LC record available at https://lccn.loc.gov/2022012397
LC ebook record available at https://lccn.loc.gov/2022012398

Printed in the United States of America

We wish to acknowledge our gratitude
for the extraordinary generosity of the
Hitz Foundation

∾

Special thanks to the Play on Shakespeare staff
Lue Douthit, CEO and Creative Director
Kamilah Long, Executive Director
Taylor Bailey, Associate Creative Director and Senior Producer
Summer Martin, Director of Operations
Amrita Ramanan as Senior Cultural Strategist and Dramaturg
Katie Kennedy, Publications Project Manager

∾

Originally commissioned by the
Oregon Shakespeare Festival
Bill Rauch, Artistic Director
Cynthia Rider, Executive Director

PLAY ON SHAKESPEARE

In 2015, the Oregon Shakespeare Festival announced a new commissioning program. It was called "Play on!: 36 playwrights translate Shakespeare." It elicited a flurry of reactions. For some people this went too far: "You can't touch the language!" For others, it didn't go far enough: "Why not new adaptations?" I figured we would be on the right path if we hit the sweet spot in the middle.

Some of the reaction was due not only to the scale of the project, but its suddenness: 36 playwrights, along with 38 dramaturgs, had been commissioned and assigned to translate 39 plays, and they were already hard at work on the assignment. It also came fully funded by the Hitz Foundation with the shocking sticker price of $3.7 million.

I think most of the negative reaction, however, had to do with the use of the word "translate." It's been difficult to define precisely. It turns out that there is no word for the kind of subtle and rigorous examination of language that we are asking for. We don't mean "word for word," which is what most people think of when they hear the word translate. We don't mean "paraphrase," either.

The project didn't begin with 39 commissions. Linguist John McWhorter's musings about translating Shakespeare is what sparked this project. First published in his 1998 book *Word on the Street* and reprinted in 2010 in *American Theatre* magazine, he notes that the "irony today is that the Russians, the French, and other people in foreign countries possess Shakespeare to a much greater extent than we do, for the simple reason that they get to enjoy Shakespeare in the language they speak."

This intrigued Dave Hitz, a long-time patron of the Oregon Shakespeare Festival, and he offered to support a project that looked at Shakespeare's plays through the lens of the English we speak today. How much has the English language changed since Shakespeare? Is it possible that there are conventions in the early modern English of Shakespeare that don't translate to us today, especially in the moment of hearing it spoken out loud as one does in the theater?

How might we "carry forward" the successful communication between actor and audience that took place 400 years ago? "Carry forward," by the way, is what we mean by "translate." It is the fourth definition of *translate* in the Oxford English Dictionary.

As director of literary development and dramaturgy at the Oregon Shakespeare Festival, I was given the daunting task of figuring out how to administer the project. I began with Kenneth Cavander, who translates ancient Greek tragedies into English. I figured that someone who does that kind of work would lend an air of seriousness to the project. I asked him how might he go about translating from the source language of early modern English into the target language of contemporary modern English?

He looked at different kinds of speech: rhetorical and poetical, soliloquies and crowd scenes, and the puns in comedies. What emerged from his tinkering became a template for the translation commission. These weren't rules exactly, but instructions that every writer was given.

First, do no harm. There is plenty of the language that doesn't need translating. And there is some that does. Every playwright had different criteria for assessing what to change.

Second, go line-by-line. No editing, no cutting, no "fixing." I want the whole play translated. We often cut the gnarly bits in

Shakespeare for performance. What might we make of those bits if we understood them in the moment of hearing them? Might we be less compelled to cut?

Third, all other variables stay the same: the time period, the story, the characters, their motivations, and their thoughts. We designed the experiment to examine the language.

Fourth, and most important, the language must follow the same kind of rigor and pressure as the original, which means honoring the meter, rhyme, rhetoric, image, metaphor, character, action, and theme. Shakespeare's astonishingly compressed language must be respected. Trickiest of all: making sure to work within the structure of the iambic pentameter.

We also didn't know which of Shakespeare's plays might benefit from this kind of investigation: the early comedies, the late tragedies, the highly poetic plays. So we asked three translators who translate plays from other languages into English to examine a Shakespeare play from each genre outlined in the *First Folio*: Kenneth took on *Timon of Athens,* a tragedy; Douglas Langworthy worked on the *Henry the Sixth* history plays, and Ranjit Bolt tried his hand at the comedy *Much Ado about Nothing.*

Kenneth's *Timon* received a production at the Alabama Shakespeare in 2014 and it was on the plane ride home that I thought about expanding the project to include 39 plays. And I wanted to do them all at once. The idea was to capture a snapshot of contemporary modern English. I couldn't oversee that many commissions, and when Ken Hitz (Dave's brother and president of the Hitz Foundation) suggested that we add a dramaturg to each play, the plan suddenly unfolded in front of me. The next day, I made a simple, but extensive, proposal to Dave on how to commission and develop 39 translations in three years. He responded immediately with "Yes."

My initial thought was to only commission translators who translate plays. But I realized that "carry forward" has other meanings. There was a playwright in the middle of the conversation 400 years ago. What would it mean to carry *that* forward?

For one thing, it would mean that we wanted to examine the texts through the lens of performance. I am interested in learning how a dramatist makes sense of the play. Basically, we asked the writers to create performable companion pieces.

I wanted to tease out what we mean by contemporary modern English, and so we created a matrix of writers who embodied many different lived experiences: age, ethnicity, gender-identity, experience with translations, geography, English as a second language, knowledge of Shakespeare, etc.

What the playwrights had in common was a deep love of language and a curiosity about the assignment. Not everyone was on board with the idea and I was eager to see how the experiment would be for them. They also pledged to finish the commission within three years.

To celebrate the completion of the translations, we produced a festival in June 2019 in partnership with The Classic Stage Company in New York to hear all 39 of them. Four hundred years ago I think we went to *hear* a play; today we often go to *see* a play. In the staged reading format of the Festival, we heard these plays as if for the first time. The blend of Shakespeare with another writer was seamless and jarring at the same time. Countless actors and audience members told us that the plays were understandable in ways they had never been before.

Now it's time to share the work. We were thrilled when Ayanna Thompson and her colleagues at the Arizona Center for Medieval and Renaissance Studies offered to publish the translations for us.

I ask that you think of these as marking a moment in time.

The editions published in this series are based on the scripts that were used in the Play on! Festival in 2019. For the purpose of the readings, there were cuts allowed and these scripts represent those reading drafts.

The original commission tasked the playwrights and dramaturg to translate the whole play. The requirement of the commission was for two drafts which is enough to put the ball in play. The real fun with these texts is when there are actors, a director, a dramaturg, and the playwright wrestling with them together in a rehearsal room.

The success of a project of this scale depends on the collaboration and contributions of many people. The playwrights and dramaturgs took the assignment seriously and earnestly and were humble and gracious throughout the development of the translations. Sally Cade Holmes and Holmes Productions, our producer since the beginning, provided a steady and calm influence.

We have worked with more than 1,200 artists in the development of these works. We have partnered with more than three dozen theaters and schools. Numerous readings and more than a dozen productions of these translations have been heard and seen in the United States as well as Canada, England, and the Czech Republic.

There is a saying in the theater that 80% of the director's job is taken care of when the production is cast well. Such was my luck when I hired Taylor Bailey, who has overseen every reading and workshop, and was the producer of the Festival in New York. Katie Kennedy has gathered all the essays, and we have been supported by the rest of the Play on Shakespeare team: Kamilah Long, Summer Martin, and Amrita Ramanan.

All of this has come to be because Bill Rauch, then artistic director of the Oregon Shakespeare Festival, said yes when Dave

Hitz pitched the idea to him in 2011. Actually he said, "Hmm, interesting," which I translated to "yes." I am dearly indebted to that 'yes.'

My gratitude to Dave, Ken, and the Hitz Foundation can never be fully expressed. Their generosity, patience, and unwavering belief in what we are doing has given us the confidence to follow the advice of Samuel Beckett: "Ever tried. Ever failed. No matter. Try again. Fail again. Fail better."

Play on!

Dr. Lue Douthit
CEO/Creative Director at Play on Shakespeare
October 2020

WHAT WAS I THINKING?

On *Edward III*
by Octavio Solis

My first encounter with William Shakespeare took place in the spring of 1974 when I was cast in my high school production of *A Midsummer Night's Dream.* The play was a horribly shortened, bowdlerized 45-minute version of the play intended for Texas University Interscholastic League competition, but for this young El Pasoan, it was a revelation. Here I was thinking I already knew all the English I needed to navigate through my life, and then this Elizabethan bard short-circuits my brain and plants the most exotic flowers in it. I couldn't believe it. I had no idea what I was saying half the time, but I loved the way those words fit in my mouth. From that moment on, I sought every play and poem Shakespeare had ever written.

I resolved to be an actor due to this experience, and I avidly studied his works in college, even traveling to London to immerse myself in his world for an entire year, attending productions of his works at the Royal Shakespeare Company, the Old Vic, the Young Vic, Riverside Studios, and the National Theatre. I found what actors loved about performing his words—the way in which the precision of language supplied all the emotional content, and how the words could be endlessly mined for meaning. But I also realized how inaccessible some of his passages were for me, and not only me, but so many English natives, my fellow students who came from the Midlands and County Kent and the London area who could hardly even unravel the most famous lines from his plays.

Clearly, I could refer to the annotations and look up the meanings, but that took the fun and immediacy out of the enjoyment of seeing the works, and who could ever remember them all? I resolved that at some level, while I reveled in the poetry, which yielded so much meaning, there would be a good percentage of his language that would always remain opaque.

When I was asked to translate one of his plays, I chose *Edward III*, chiefly because I was curious about this play, which I hadn't even known was part of the canon, but also because I was certain that no one else would recognize the work either and wouldn't give two figs for the damage I might do it. I was that nervous about the assignment. But working on this obscure play gave me some insight into what exactly caused my brain to blur sometimes when listening to Shakespeare and offered even further insights into the genius of the man himself. While at first I had pained over the opening speech of *Edward III* for two weeks, something took hold of my comprehension and suddenly I was gliding over the rest of the acts with ease. The anxiety over translating this difficult work turned to the kind of delight I hadn't felt since discovering the Midsummer idioms of 1974.

Edward III is a history play, perhaps Shakespeare's first depicting the royal line of Britain, and as such, laid before me the beginning of the Hundred Years' War between England and France, and on that level alone, the play was fascinating. There was the siege of Calais, even the Burghers immortalized by Rodin; there was Edward "the Black Prince" ripping through the fields of battle as he earned his knighthood; there were the battles themselves, the *naval* Battle of Sluys and the Battle of Crécy; and there was the long-rumored romance between the King and the Countess of Salisbury; all of these happening about 800 years ago and yet feeling utterly contemporary in the Bard's hands. But very quickly I became aware of the passages and lines that I always seemed to stumble on.

These often had to do with expressions no longer common among English-speakers today or referred to jokes and events that have no meaning beyond the age that produced them. There were words that, for good or ill, have fallen completely out of use: terms for appurtenances of battle and horsemanship and heraldry. These had to be simplified to keep the viewer (and the reader) from falling off the flow of the language. I did the same with "thee" and "thine" and "sayeth," translating these into "you" and "your" and "say."

There were passages that were utterly baffling to me, which I had to research through so many annotations. For instance, there was a speech by Edward that made no sense unless I knew that in Elizabethan times, the assumed wisdom was that the human eye had its own light source that radiated out during nighttime, like the beam of a flashlight. And there was a reference to the commonly accepted notion that the nightingale sang its most beautiful song when it deliberately slashed its chest against the thorns of the briar. No one believes either of these conceptions today, and few even realize they were held as facts back then, and so I had to accommodate by translating the sense of these in another way.

At times, I felt Shakespeare was showing off his knowledge of classical and Biblical literature that I am certain riveted audiences at the Globe but leave so many today scratching their heads. There were obscure allusions to passages from Ovid's *Metamorphoses*, Hero and Leander, and Judith severing the head of Holofernes. These required some trimming and elucidation, since so much of our education skirts these long-hallowed texts. (I only know about Holofernes's decapitation from Artemisia Gentileschi's famous painting.)

But even as I pruned the garden of this lush language in *Edward III*, I maintained the poetry. Shakespeare's performative idiom requires people to work at it; one must listen, and the quality of listening must be keen. I didn't cheapen or "dumb down" the lyricism or the various literary tropes he employs. There are extended metaphors and symbols, the use of alliteration, chiasmus, irony, oxymorons, and rhetorical devices. I tried to adhere to the meter as much as possible, and preserved the rhyme, even with different words in place. My aim in this project was to make myself invisible in the process, to sound as much like Shakespeare as possible, that is, to translate the work as the Bard himself would have done it had he been here today.

That is where the revelation of his genius laid itself bare to me. I used my trusty Roget's on the bookshelf and Thesaurus.com on my computer and all the online lexicons at my disposal for my translation, including the other editions of *Edward III* with their annotations and all of Shakespeare's other works, to boot. Shakespeare had none of this. There wasn't even an *Oxford English Dictionary* in existence yet. He wrote this play and all the others using only the texts that he studied and the common and uncommon vernacular of the people of his day. When he needed a word to fit the scansion and it wasn't readily available to him, he simply made it up. I can't recount how many times I looked in the annotations section of my *Edward III* edition and read "first written use of this word" or "first use of this term." Imagine how many other words and expressions he invented in his entire canon. English was a living organism in his hands and it's a credit to his age that, when his characters spoke these words for the first time, audiences knew exactly what he meant. Words get added to the dictionary all the time today from many different sources, but rarely do they come from a single source like they did with Shakespeare.

For all of Shakespeare's genius, I was struck by how unpedantic a poet he was. He wrote *Edward III* entirely in verse, employing iambs within a line of five metrical feet. Weak, strong, weak, strong, weak, strong, weak, strong, weak, strong. He adhered to this pattern with rigor, but as I strove to translate this work, I found that he cheated. Sometimes he only included nine syllables in a line; sometimes there were eleven; sometimes even twelve. He always seemed to make up for it with enjambment, that is, continuing the flow and sense of the line into the ensuing line, where he would add a foot there was that missing in the prior line, but not always. He understood that audiences weren't going to be counting the meter to be sure he was accurate, they were going to be watching the play and feeling the meter inside themselves. So what if a beat was missing? Who cares about that when the Battle of Crécy is raging? I took my cue from him and designed my translation tempos based on his own beat variations within *Edward III*.

There is no reason any part of Shakespeare's plays needs to be opaque; we don't ever have to settle for "getting the gist" when we could be getting it all. We don't have to be looking up all the terms and words and expressions we don't understand prior to a performance of his works. Every country has translated his canon into their own language; that's essentially what we are doing here. Still, I hope my translation of *Edward III* offers clarity and force where the original cannot, and failing that, perhaps some renewed attention to the original itself. It is a marvel of a play.

Octavio Solis
August 2021

CHARACTERS IN THE PLAY

(in order of speaking)

KING EDWARD III, King of England
ROBERT, COUNT OF ARTOIS
LORD AUDLEY
DUKE OF LORRAINE
PRINCE EDWARD, the Black Prince; King Edward's son
EARL OF WARWICK, the Countess of Salisbury's father
SIR WILLIAM MONTAGUE, the Earl of Salisbury's nephew
THE COUNTESS OF SALISBURY, the Earl of Salisbury's wife
KING DAVID, the King of Scotland, part of the Bruce Clan
SIR WILLIAM DOUGLAS, a Scottish nobleman
LODOWICK, King Edward's secretary
EARL OF DERBY
KING JOHN II, the King of France
PRINCE CHARLES, Duke of Normandy, King John's son
KING OF BOHEMIA, a supporter of the French
POLONIAN CAPTAIN
MARINER
PRINCE PHILIP, King John's youngest son
ONE, a French citizen
TWO, a French citizen
THREE, a French citizen
WOMAN, a French citizen
FRENCHMAN
GOBIN DE GRACE, a French prisoner
LORD MOUNTFORD, Duke of Brittany
EARL OF SALISBURY

CAST OF CHARACTERS

VILLIERS, a Norman lord

POOR FRENCHMAN

LORD PERCY

CAPTAIN, a French captain

HERALDS

CITIZEN ONE, a citizen of Calais

CITIZEN TWO, a citizen of Calais

QUEEN PHILIPPA, King Edward's wife

COPELAND, a squire

Other Messengers, Danish Troops, Soldiers, French Citizens, two **Children**, and two **Esquires**

ACT 1 ◆ SCENE 1

Enter King Edward, Derby, Prince Edward, Audley,
Warwick, and Artois

KING

Robert of Artois, banished you have been
From France your native country, but with us
You will retain no less authority
As herewith Earl of Richmond you shall be,
So let us now discuss our pedigree.   5
Who next succeeded Philip le Beau?

ARTOIS

Three sons of his which all successfully
Did sit upon their father's regal throne
Yet died and left no issue of their loins.

KING

Was not my mother sister to those sons?   10

ARTOIS

She was, my lord, the sister Isabel,
The only daughter that King Philip had
Whom afterwards your father took to wife
And from whose fragrant garden of her womb
Were you thus born the flower of Europe's hope,   15
True inheritor to the crown of France.
But oh, the rancor of rebellious minds,
When they of this new royal lineage learned,
The French obscured your mother's privilege
And, though she is the next of blood, proclaimed   20
John of the House of Valois now their king.
The reason they give is the realm of France

1

Ample with princes of great parentage
Should no pretender place upon the throne
Unless he be descended from the male   25
And that's the only ground of their contempt
By which they are excluding you as heir,
But soon they'll find their falsified ground
To be but dusty heaps of brittle sand.
No doubt they think it is a heinous thing   30
That I, a Frenchman, would divulge their aim
But heaven has a record of my vows
And knows it is not hate nor private wrong
But love of country that accords my tongue
The right to give so detailed a report.   35
While you well guard the lineage of our peace
This John of Valois indirectly climbs.
What choice have we but to embrace our king?
How better demonstrate our duty than
By striving to repulse this tyrant's pride   40
And dub you the shepherd of our commonwealth?
KING
Your words, Artois, like most productive rain
Do nourish the growth of my esteem
And with their sunny vigor engender
Hot courage within this my noble breast   45
Which up till now was racked in ignorance
But now rises up on glory's golden wing
To press the birthright of fair Isabel
With steel upon the stubborn necks of those
Who dare deny my sovereignty in France.   50
(sound a horn)
A messenger! Lord Audley, see him here.
                              Enter a Messenger with Lorraine

AUDLEY

    The Duke of Lorraine having crossed the seas

    Begs special conference with your highness.

KING

    Admit him Lords that we may hear the news.

    Speak, Duke of Lorraine, what cause brings you here?   55

LORRAINE

    The most renowned and right King John of France

    Does send his greetings and by me commands

    That since only through his generous nature

    The Guyenne Dukedom was conferred to you,

    You, Edward owe him due homage for it.   60

    And for that purpose do I summon you

    To go to France within these forty days

    So that according to the custom there

    You may pronounce allegiance to our king

    Or your claim in the province is revoked   65

    And he himself will repossess the place.

KING

    See how swiftly Fortune laughs in my face!

    No sooner advised to prepare for France

    Than straightaway I am invited, no,

    With penalty threatened if I don't come!   70

    It would be churlish to deny him thus.

    Lorraine, here's the answer to your king:

    I mean to visit him as he requests.

    Not like a vassal bent upon his knees

    But like a conqueror to make him bow.   75

    Tell him the crown that he usurps is mine

    And where he sets his foot he ought to kneel.

    It's not his petty dukedom that I claim

    But all the whole dominions of the realm

3

Which if he grudgingly refuses me   80
I'll pluck the haughty plumes he struts with
And send him naked to the wilderness.

LORRAINE

Then, Edward, with respect to all your lords
I do pronounce defiance to your face.

PRINCE

Defiance, Frenchman? That word we heave back   85
Even to the bottom of your master's throat,
And though you speak with reverence to these
Our lords and to my father, gracious king,
I think it false, I think it scurrilous,
And him that sent you an infertile kite   90
Buzzing over the nest of eagles
From which we'll shake him with so rough a storm
That others by his harm will be warned.

WARWICK

Tell him the lion's mane is not for him,
For if he meets the lion in the field   95
He will be ripped to pieces for his pride.

ARTOIS

The soundest counsel I can give his grace
Is to concede the fight he's sure to lose.
Less scorn is due confessing a mistake
Than from the judgment suffered for its sake.   100

LORRAINE

Degenerate traitor, viper to the place
That gave you life and your enrichèd youth!
Are you a part of this conspiracy?

The King draws his sword

KING

Lorraine, behold the sharpness of this sword.

4

The longing that presses against my heart   105
Is sharper and more vexing than this blade
And like the nightingale's penetrating song
Will cut the fiber of my sleep to shreds
Until the English flag is raised in France.
This is my final answer, so be gone.   110

LORRAINE

Neither steel nor any English bluster
Afflicts my senses like the sight of you,
Who turned so false yet should have been most true.

Exit Lorraine

KING

Thus, lords, we set our battleships to sea
Our pledge is made and war is soon begun   115
But not so quickly nor so eas'ly won.

Enter Montague

But look, here comes Sir William Montague.
How stands the pact between the Scot and us?

MONTAGUE

Cracked and dissevered, my renownèd lord.
The treacherous king no sooner was informed   120
Of the withdrawal of your northern force
But in breach of his former oath to you
Assaulted foully all the border towns.
And now the tyrant Scot has besieged
Roxbury Castle where in her confinement   125
The Countess Salisbury is likely to die.

KING

That is your daughter, Warwick, is it not?
Whose husband served in Brittany for so long
Defending the rule of Lord Mountford there?

WARWICK

It is, my Lord. 130

KING

First, therefore Audley this I charge you with:
Recruit the footmen for our wars in France
And Ned, you muster up our men at arms,
In every shire enlist as many bands
You can of soldiers of a lusty spirit 135
That will dread nothing but dishonor's blot.
Be wary, my lords, since we do commence
A widespread war against a mighty nation.
But sirs, be resolute! We shall have wars
On every side, and Ned resolve you now 140
To put aside your books and bookish ways
And brace your shoulders for the armor's weight.

PRINCE

Exhilarating to my youthful blood
This talk of broiling war and tumult is,
Like at the coronation of a king 145
When the joyful clamors of the people
Pronounce aloud the words "Hail Caesar! Hail!"
Within this school of honor I shall learn
To either sacrifice my foes to death
Or heave in worthy combat my last breath. 150
Then jubilance lead us each our own way!
These great affairs cannot afford delay!

Exit

ACT 1 ◆ SCENE 2

Enter the Countess

COUNTESS

Pathetic how my eyes still search in vain

For any lifeline from my sovereign lord.
Ah, cousin Montague, I feel you lack
The fiery forceful spirit to entreat
With fervent heart the king on my behalf.   5
Impossible for you to phrase the grief
That I endure as hostage to this Scot
Who'll either woo me with most unwelcome
Gabble or force his barbarous ways on me.

Enter David and Douglas with Lorraine

I must hold back, my everlasting foe   10
Approaches there. I'll step aside but close
To catch their brutish babble, blunt and gross.

KING DAVID

My Lord of Lorraine, to our brother in France
Commend us as the King of Christendom
That we owe reverence to and love as well.   15
As for your delegation, sir, return
And say that we with England never parley
Nor make with them fair weather or beg truce
But burn their nearby towns and light our way
Down eager raids toward their city York.   20
Farewell, and tell him that you met us here
Before this castlekeep; and say you left
As it submitted even to our will.

LORRAINE

I take my leave, and will gladly convey
This gratifying message to my King.   25

Exit Lorraine

KING DAVID

Now Douglas to our former task again
For the division of these latest spoils.

7

DOUGLAS

My liege, I crave the lady and no more.

KING DAVID

Nay, no more of that, first I make the choice
And first do I lay claim to her myself.   30

DOUGLAS

Why, then, my liege, let me finger her jewels.

KING DAVID

Those are her own and what's her own is mine
As who inherits her inherits all.

Enter a Scot in haste

MESSENGER

My liege, as we were riding on the hills
To fetch our plunder thereabouts we saw   35
Or think we might have seen an armored horde.
The sun reflecting on the armor showed
A field of steel, a forestfull of pikes.
Your highness, quickly fit your mind to this!
A four hour's march or sooner will bring   40
Both field and forest to this place, my liege!

KING DAVID

Pull back! Retreat! It is the King of England!

DOUGLAS

Jemmy, my man, saddle my bonny black!

KING DAVID

You mean to fight? But, Douglas, we're outmanned.

DOUGLAS

I call my horse to fight naught but to flee!   45

COUNTESS

My lords of Scotland, will you stay and drink?

KING DAVID

She's mocking us, Douglas, I will not abide it.

COUNTESS

    Remind me, which is he must have the lady

    And which her jewels? I am sure my lords

    Will not depart till you have shared the spoils.   50

KING DAVID

    She heard the messenger and knows our talk;

    Now this reversal makes her jeer at us.

Enter another Messenger

MESSENGER II

    They're coming armed, my lord! We're overwhelmed!

COUNTESS

    Do catch the French ambassador, my liege,

    And tell him that you dare not ride to York.   55

    Advise him that your bonny horse is lame!

KING DAVID

    She heard that too? Intolerable grief!

    Woman, be still. Although I do not stay —

COUNTESS

    It's not for fear, and yet you run away.

Exit Scots

    O sweet redemption! Welcome to our house!   60

    The arrogant and boisterous-boasting Scot

    That swore before my walls he'd not retreat

    Against the greatest army of the land,

    With faceless fear that always turns his back

    Turned tail against the blasting northeast wind   65

    At the mere mention and report of arms.

Enter Montague

    O summer's day! My cousin here at last!

MONTAGUE

    How are you, aunt? We're not the Scots,

    Why do you shut your gates against your friends?

COUNTESS

Well may you have a hearty welcome, nephew,   70

For you come chasing my foes well away.

MONTAGUE

The king himself in person will appear.

Come, dear aunt, congratulate his highness.

COUNTESS

How may I entertain his majesty

To show my duty to his honored grace?   75

Exit

Enter King Edward, Warwick, Artois, with others

KING EDWARD

What, are the stealing foxes fled and gone

Before we could set our dogs upon them?

WARWICK

They are, my liege, but with bays of triumph

Hot and hardy hounds chase them at the heels.

Enter the Countess

KING EDWARD

This is the Countess, Warwick, is she not?   80

WARWICK

My daughter, sire, whose beauty has with dread

Been sullied, withered, plucked up and blown

Like a May blossom in pernicious winds.

KING EDWARD

You say she has been fairer than she is?

WARWICK

My gracious king, fair I would not call her,   85

But only compared to the Countess before

Which is the Countess that I know the more.

KING EDWARD *(aside)*

What beguilement must have lurked in her eyes

10

When they surpassed their own surpassing charms,
That even dimmed in her decline, their gaze 90
Now draws my gaze past piercing majesty
To this unvarnished beauty I now see.
COUNTESS
In duty lower than the ground I kneel
And for my dull knees bow my feeling heart
To witness my obedience to your highness 95
With many millions of my fondest thanks
For this your royal presence whose approach
Has driven war and danger from my gate.
KING EDWARD
Good lady, rise, I come to offer peace
Although for it I have purchased war. 100
COUNTESS
No war to you, my liege, the Scots are gone
And gallop home toward Scotland with their spite.
KING EDWARD *(aside)*
Before I pine and pitch for shameful love —
(aloud)
Come, we'll pursue the Scots. Artois, away!
COUNTESS
A little while, my gracious savior, stay 105
And let the power of a mighty king
Honor our roof. My husband on the front
When he hears of it will exult for pride.
KING EDWARD
Pardon me, Countess. I will come no near'r;
I dreamt last night of treason and I fear. 110
COUNTESS
Far from us may this ugly treason lie!

KING EDWARD *(aside)*

    If eyes to see by render their own light

    And light of day itself expands my sight,

    Then gazing here I should but cannot see,

    For her twin suns steal my own light from me.   115

(aloud)

    Warwick, Artois, our horses, let's away!

COUNTESS

    What might I speak to make my sovereign stay?

KING EDWARD *(aside)*

    What tongue can say more than your speaking eye

    But everything my heart would verify?

COUNTESS

    Don't pass your presence like the April sun   120

    Which warms our earth then all too soon is done.

    Your gladness laid upon our outer wall

    Would doubly grace us in our banquet hall.

    To relish this, I beg your majesty

    To beg yourself to stay awhile with me.   125

KING EDWARD

    Countess, though my business urges me

    It will wait while I stay awhile with thee.

    Come on, my lords, I am her guest tonight.

Exit

ACT 2 ◆ SCENE 1

Enter Lodowick

LODOWICK

I think I see his eye in her eye lost,
His ear drunk on her sweet tongue's utterance,
His changing passions, like inconstant clouds
That rack upon the carriage of the winds,
Flush, rush, and die in his uneasy cheeks.   5
She blushed, and even then did he look pale
As if her cheeks by magical exchange
Attracted all the cherry blood from his.
If she did blush, it's merely modesty
Being in the sacred presence of a king.   10
If he did blush, it's some unspoken shame
That veils the eyes of this immodest king.
Farewell you Scottish wars, you're nothing to
The lasting English siege of peevish love.
Here comes his Highness walking all alone.   15

Enter King Edward

KING EDWARD

She was fair before, but fairer since I've come,
With every added word her voice more silver,
Her wit more witty. Like that strange account
She relayed of meeting David and his Scots.
She said "Like so he spoke," then spoke the brogue   20
With epithets and accents of the Scot
But somewhat better than the Scot could speak!
"And so," she said, and answered in her voice
For who could speak like her but she herself?

13

When she spoke of peace I thought her tongue 25
Sent War itself to prison, and her talk
Of War I swear stirred Caesar from his grave
To hear War beautified by her discourse.
Wisdom is folly on any tongue but hers,
Beauty a crime on any face not hers, 30
No summer come except in her delight,
Nor frosty winter save in her disdain.
I cannot blame the Scots who did besiege her,
For she is all the treasure of our land,
But call them cowards that they ran away 35
From such a rich and lovely cause to stay.
Is that you, Lodowick? Bring me ink and paper.

LODOWICK

I will, my lord.

KING EDWARD

And bid the Lords their chess game keep in play
As time will meditate with us alone. 40

LODOWICK

I will, my sovereign.

Exit Lodowick

KING EDWARD

This fellow is well read in poetry
And has a lusty and persuasive spirit.
I will acquaint him with my passion
Which he will lyric into woven veils 45
Through which this Venus queen shall see
That she's the muse of my infirmity.

Enter Lodowick

KING EDWARD

Have you some ink and paper ready, Lodowick?

14

LODOWICK

I don't quite have the period on her praise. —

KING EDWARD

— Because her praise is never finished, sir,   105
But infinite, as boundless as my love —
Then why do you bring up the period
For what commands unending adoration?
Read, let us hear.

LODOWICK

"More fair and chaste than Dian of the moon … "   110

KING EDWARD

That line has two faults gross and palpable.
You liken her to the pale queen of night
Who being set in dark seems therefore bright?
What is she, when the sun lifts up his head
But a fading taper dim and dead?   115
My dear will gaze at heaven's eye at noon,
Outshine the golden sun and make it swoon.

LODOWICK

What is the other fault, my sovereign lord?

KING EDWARD

Read me the line again.

LODOWICK

"Fair and chaste as —"   120

KING EDWARD

Why glorify her treasured chastity,
When it will shackle my pursuit of her?
Sir, I would rather have her chased than chaste.
Out with the moon line, I'll have none of it
But let me have her likened to the sun;   125
Say that her splendor's thrice that of the sun,
That her perfections outperfect the sun,

17

That her rays do nourish like the sun,
Proclaim her free and lavish as the sun.
Let's see what follows that same moonlight line. 130

LODOWICK

"More fair and chaste than Dian of the moon,
More bold in her devotion — "

KING EDWARD

Than whom, do tell?

LODOWICK

"Than Judith was."

KING EDWARD

O Monstrous! Am I then Holofernes 135
That by the next line, she'll cut off my head?
Cut the line instead! Let us hear the next.

LODOWICK

That's all I have so far.

KING EDWARD

Thank you then for doing little damage
Though the little there is damaging enough. 140
No, let the soldier talk of boist'rous war,
Love cannot sing except on lover's tongues.
Give me the pen and paper, I will write —

Enter Countess

But look, here comes the keeper of my spirit.
Lod'wick, this is no way to draw a battle! 145
These wings, these flankers, and these squadrons
Betray your lack of tactical arts.
You should have placed this here, this other there.

COUNTESS

Pardon my boldness, my most gracious lords,
Consider this intrusion duty-bound 150
For I come to see how my sovereign fares.

KING EDWARD

    Redraw the lines as I described here, go.

LODOWICK

    My lord.

Exit

COUNTESS

    I am sorry to see my liege so sad.

    How may I dispel this melancholy,   155

    This much too sullen consort, from your side?

KING EDWARD

    Ah, lady, bluntly put, I cannot strew

    The flowers of solace in a ground of shame.

    Since coming here, good Countess, I've been wronged.

COUNTESS

    Oh God forbid someone in my house   160

    Should do my sovereign wrong! Kind-hearted king

    Acquaint me with your cause of discontent!

KING EDWARD

    What good or remedy would it do now?

COUNTESS

    As much, my liege, as all my woman's power

    Can pawn itself to purchase peace for you.   165

KING EDWARD

    If you mean it, then my redress is here.

    Induce your power to redeem my joys

    And I am joyful, Countess, or else lost.

COUNTESS

    I will, my liege.

KING EDWARD

    Swear, Countess. Swear you will.   170

COUNTESS

    By heaven I will.

KING EDWARD

    Then take a step somewhat outside yourself

    To tell yourself a king somewhat admires you;

    And that within you all the power lies

    To make him happy, and that you have sworn   175

    To give him all the joy within your power.

    Say this and then your king will be content.

COUNTESS

    All said and done, my esteemèd sovereign.

    That power of love that I have power to give

    Is yours with all devout obedience: 180

    Employ me as you wish in proof thereof.

KING EDWARD

    You heard how fondly I admire you.

COUNTESS

    If it's my beauty that you wish, take it:

    What little I have, I prize even less.

    If it's my virtue you require, take that,   185

    For virtue that I give gives me back more.

    Whatever I possess that I may grant,

    And you may need, here freely I bequeath.

KING EDWARD

    It is your beauty that I would enjoy.

COUNTESS

    O, were it only paint, I'd wipe it off   190

    And dispossess myself of it for you.

    But, sovereign, it is soldered to my life:

    Take one and you take both, for beauty's just

    The humble shadow of my shining life.

KING EDWARD

    You could loan it for pleasure's sake awhile.   195

COUNTESS

    You may as well be loaned this heart and soul

    Yet keep my empty body still alive,

    As pawn my body off without the soul

    That governs it, yet keep my soul unspoiled.

    My flesh is bower, court and abbey to   200

    The pure residing angel of my soul;

    If her estate I should to you decree

    I kill my poor soul, my poor soul me.

KING EDWARD

    Did you not swear to grant me what I would?

COUNTESS

    I did, my liege, to grant you what I could.   205

KING EDWARD

    I want no more of you than you'll allow

    Nor will I beg to you, but rather buy —

    Yes, buy your love, and for the payment due

    I'll tender all my tender love to you.

COUNTESS

    If your lips were not sanctified, my lord,   210

    You would profane them with the words you speak.

    The love you offer me you cannot give,

    Since Caesar owes that tribute to his queen.

    The love you beg of me I cannot give,

    Since Sarah owes her Abraham that due.   215

    The counterfeit who pays with his false coin

    Pays with his life, my lord; will you so dare

    Commit highest treason against our God

    And stamp his Word on pleas prohibited

    While your oath and allegiance are forgot?   220

    In violating wedlock's sacred law

    You break a greater honor in yourself.

It's lesser privilege to be crowned a king
Than to take a wedding vow: your forebear,
Lonely reigning Adam in his domain,   225
By God was not anointed for a king
But crowned by him with marriage to his wife.
It is civil crime to break your statutes,
Which by your sovereign hand you would not do;
How much worse to defile this holy act   230
Made by the mouth of God, sealed with His hand?
I know, my liege, you try my husband's love,
Who does you loyal service in your wars,
By testing me, the wife of Salisbury,
With hearing of a whore and lecher's tale.   235
Should your Grace judge me guilty if I stay,
From that, and not from you, I turn away.

Exit

KING EDWARD

Is it her beauty that makes her voice divine
Or is her voice sweet chaplain to her beauty?
Just as the wind will beautify a sail   240
And as a sail becomes the unseen wind,
So does her voice beauty, and beauty voice.
If only she were free as air to me!
Why, so she is; for when my arms embrace her,
This I do and catch nothing but myself.   245
I have to have her, for I cannot beat
With reason and reproof my love away.

Enter Warwick

Here comes her father: I will work with him
To plant my banner in this field of love.

WARWICK

How is it that my sovereign is so sad?   250

22

May I with your indulgence know your grief,
For if I have the means within my power
I'll liberate you from it, good my lord.

KING EDWARD

How kind and unsolicited a gift
That I too boldly would have asked of you.   255
But O, you world, wet nurse of flattery,
Why do you tip men's tongues with words of gold
And anvil down their deeds with heavy lead
That fair performance cannot follow promise?

WARWICK

Far be it from the honor of my age   260
That I should owe you gold and pay you lead:
I'm too old and cynical to flatter.
I say again: that if I knew your grief
And that by me it might be lessened,
What harm's in that, my lord, which does you good?   265

KING EDWARD

These are the tendered vagaries of liars,
That never pay the duty of their words.
You won't delay to swear by what you've said,
But once you've heard the nature of my grief
This vilely gurgled vomit of your word   270
You'll lap up once again; and leave me worse.

WARWICK

By God, I won't! Not even if, my lord,
You make me run into your sword and die.

KING EDWARD

What if my grief is no way treatable
But by the breach and losing of your honor?   275

WARWICK

If loss of honor will benefit you,

23

I'll count that loss to my benefit too.
KING EDWARD
　　You think you can unswear your pledge to me?
WARWICK
　　I can't, my lord, nor would I if I could.
KING EDWARD
　　But if you did, what should I say to you?　　　　　　　　280
WARWICK
　　What I would say to any perjurer
　　That breaks the sacred warrant of an oath.
KING EDWARD
　　Say what you'd say to him that broke his oath!
WARWICK
　　Fool, you have broken faith with God and man
　　And by them excommunicated stand.　　　　　　　　285
KING EDWARD
　　What kind of duty would befit a man
　　Who breaks a legal and religious vow?
WARWICK
　　A duty for the devil, not for man.
KING EDWARD
　　That devil's duty must you do for me,
　　Or break your oath and cancel all the bonds　　　　　　290
　　Of love and duty that you share with me.
　　And therefore, Warwick, if you're who you say,
　　The lord and master of your solemn word,
　　Go to your daughter and on my behalf
　　Command her, woo her, win her any way　　　　　　　300
　　To be my mistress and my secret love.
　　I will not stay since you have no reply:
　　Her oath your oath must break, or I will die.
　　　　　　　　　　Exit King

24

WARWICK

O doting King! O detestable duty!
By doing right myself I may wrong myself 305
Since I made a vow in the name of God
To break a vow made in the name of God.
What if I swear by this right hand to cut
The right hand off? Much better to defy
The statute I swear by than depose it. 310
But neither will I do: I'll keep my word
And to my daughter make a recantation
Of all the virtue I have preached to her.
I'll say bear in mind his Highness's embrace
But never forsake your Salisbury's arms; 315
I'll say an oath is easily broken,
But broken, not so easily pardoned;
I'll say it is true charity to love,
But not true love to be so charitable;
I'll say his crown will overrule shame, 320
But mark how shame will rule over the crown;
I'll say it is my duty to persuade,
But hers is not to be persuaded thus.
                    Enter the Countess
She's here! Did any father ever have
To serve his King against his child's behalf? 325

COUNTESS

My lord and father, I have sought for you.
My mother and the others summon you
To stay near the presence of his majesty
And do your best to make his highness merry.

WARWICK *(aside)*

How do I start this gross ungodliness? 330

25

(to the Countess)

Since you're no daughter nor my dear friend's wife,
I'm not the Warwick that you take me for,
But an attorney from the court of hell
Who's taken residence in this body's house
To bear a message to you from the King.   335
The mighty King of England longs for you:
He with the power to take away your life
Has power to take your honor; so consent
To pawn your honor rather than your life.
Honor is often lost and won again,   340
The King with glory will cover your shame;
And if they find you out, he'll dazzle them
With splendor so they never doubt of you.
The king's great name will temper your small vice
And give the bitter potion of reproach   345
A sugared sweet and most delicious taste.
Besides, there is no harm in doing that
Which without shame could not be left undone.
Thus have I in his majesty's behalf
Dressed the vice in metaphoric virtue   350
And now await your answer to his suit.

COUNTESS

Unnatural! Again besieged! O me,
To have escaped the danger of my foes
Only to be ten times worse beset by friends!
Has he no other means to taint my blood   355
Except by drafting my blood's fountainhead
To play his shameless and vile advocate?
No wonder the branch becomes infected,
When poison has polluted the root;
No wonder that the leprous infant dies   360

When there's venom on the nurse's teat.
Why then, give sin a license to sin more
And youth the slack reins of debauchery;
Forbid the strict forbidding of the law,
And cancel every rule that levies shame   365
For shameful acts, and penance for offense.
No, let me die, if his too wanton pride
Will have it so, before I will consent
To be an actor in his graceless lust.

WARWICK

Why, now you speak as I would have you speak;   370
And mark how I unsay my words for you:
An honorable grave is more esteemed
Than the polluted bedsheets of a king;
The greater the heart, the greater the cause,
Be it good or bad, that it undertakes;   375
All these maxims and yet more I would place
Between his satisfaction and your shame:
That poison blackens in a golden cup;
Dark night seems darker by the lightning flash;
Lilies that fester smell far worse than weeds;   380
And those high-blooded men inclined to vice
Will be laid lower than the vice itself.
So here's my blessing bosomed in you, child,
Which to heavy curse will turn
When you turn from your honor's golden name   385
To that black cult of bed-defiling shame.

COUNTESS

I'll follow you; and when my mind is turned
My soul and body will by shame be burned.

Exit

27

ACT 2 ◆ SCENE 2

Enter at one door Derby from France
at another door Audley with a drum

DERBY

O noble Audley! No man better met!

How is it with our Edward and his peers?

AUDLEY

It's been a fortnight since I saw him last,

That time he sent me forth to muster men,

Which I accordingly have lined up here   5

To impress his Highness with their number.

Good news, my lord of Derby, from Germany?

DERBY

As good as we hoped for: the Emperor

Has rendered martial aid unto our force,

And makes our king lieutenant-general   10

In all his lands and large dominions.

Now *voilà*! for the spacious bounds of France!

AUDLEY

Indeed! Is he not pleased to hear this news?

DERBY

I have not found him yet to share them.

The King is in his chamber, discontent   15

With what I cannot tell, but he ordered

That after dinner none should interrupt him.

The Countess Salisbury and her father Warwick,

Artois and all, have trouble in their looks.

AUDLEY

Undoubtedly then something is amiss.   20

Enter the King

DERBY

Our sovereign's wish to sovereign truth become!

KING EDWARD

Ah, pity you're no witch to make it so!

DERBY

The Emperor sends greetings — *(presenting letters)*

KING EDWARD

If only they were hers …

DERBY

And has agreed upon your highness's suit —   25

KING EDWARD

Liar, she hasn't; though I wish she would.

AUDLEY

All love and duty to my lord the King!

KING EDWARD

Well, all the love but one. — What news with you?

AUDLEY

I mustered, my liege, those horse and foot soldiers

As you commanded and arrayed them here.   30

KING EDWARD

Then let the feet trudge where horses will march,

For I dismiss them all to go; begone —

Derby, I'll read into the Countess's mind.

DERBY

The Countess's mind, my liege?

KING EDWARD

I mean the Emperor. — Leave me alone.   35

AUDLEY

What's on his mind?

DERBY

Best leave him to his humor.

Exit

KING EDWARD

Thus from the heart's abundance I misspoke:

Said "Countess" for "Emperor" — and why not?
She's imperial over me and I 40
Her kneeling minion that relies upon
The pleasure or displeasure of her eye.

Enter Lodowick

What words does greater Cleopatra say
To Caesar now?

LODOWICK

That when night falls, my liege, 45
She will resolve your majesty.

KING EDWARD

What drum is this that thunders out this beat
To rouse up tender Cupid in my bosom?
Poor tissue, how it brawls against the drummer!
Go! Pound! Tear through the parchment of my heart, 50
And I will teach you to conduct sweet lines
Of poetry for the bosom of a nymph
Since I will use my heart as writing paper,
And so convert it from a scolding drumbeat
To a song of love's epistles sung 55
Between a goddess and her doting king.
Away!

Exit Lodowick

The duel I undertake requires no arms
But these of mine; and these shall meet my foe
In a deep fall of penetrating groans; 60
My eyes shall be my arrows, and the wind
They glide upon will be my heaving sighs
To whirl away my lips' artillery.
What now?

Enter Lodowick

LODOWICK

My liege, the drum that strikes the lively roll   65
Announces Prince Edward, your valiant son.

Enter Prince Edward

KING EDWARD *(aside)*

I see the boy. O, how his mother's face,
Modeled in his, corrects my strayed desire,
Berates my heart, and chides my greedy eye,
Which, being rich enough with seeing her,   70
Yet looks for more: the basest theft is that
Which can't use poverty as an excuse. —

(aloud)

Now, boy, what news?

PRINCE EDWARD

I have assembled, my dear lord and father,
The choicest buds of all our English blood   75
For our affairs to France, and here we come
To take direction from your majesty.

KING EDWARD *(aside)*

Still do I see in him the markings of
His mother's face: those eyes of his are hers,
Whose wistful looks on me do make me blush,   80
As sin against itself will testify.
Lust is a fire, and men like beacons show
The burning want within, even through their skin.
Away, you loose and fickle vanity!
Shall the large estate of fair Brittany   85
Be won by me, yet I will master not
This Edward, this little mansion of myself?
Steel me with eternal fortitude!
I go to conquer kings; yet will this king not
Subdue himself and be his enemies' fool?   90

31

I can't allow it! — Come, boy, here, advance!
Let's with our colors spice the air of France.

Enter Lodowick

LODOWICK

My liege, the Countess with a smiling air
Desires to call upon your majesty.

KING EDWARD *(aside)*

Well, there it goes! That very smile of hers   95
Has granted France reprieve and set the King,
The Dauphin, and the peers on their parole. —

(aloud)

Go, leave me, Ned, and revel with your friends.

Exit Prince

(aside)

Your mother is black-eyed like you, and you
Remind me how unfond of her I am. —   100

(aloud)

Go, usher forth the Countess on your hand,

Exit Lodowick

And let her chase away these winter clouds
For she lends beauty to sky and earth alike.
The sin is more to hack and hew at men
Than to hold in another husband's bed   105
This loveliness, this paragon unmatched
Since Adam's day to this very hour.

Enter Countess and Lodowick

Go, Lod'wick, dip your hand into your coins,
Play, spend, give, riot, drink, do as you like
Just so you go awhile and leave us be.   110

Exit Lodowick

Now my soul's playfellow, do you come
To utter that far more heavenly "yes"

To my proposal for your beauteous charms?
COUNTESS
   My father with his blessing has advised me —
KING EDWARD
   That you should yield to me?   115
COUNTESS
   As, my liege, you are due.
KING EDWARD
   And that, O dearest love, is no less due
   Than my right for right, rendered love for love.
COUNTESS
   Or wrong for wrong and endless hate for hate.
   But since I see your majesty so intent   120
   That my unwillingness, my husband's love,
   Your high rank, and my personal respect
   Are no help to me, but that your crown
   Will overrule and quash these dear regards,
   I bind my discontent to my content   125
   And what I won't do, I'll compel to do,
   Provided you yourself remove those blocks
   That stand between your Highness's love and mine.
KING EDWARD
   Name them, fair Countess, and by heaven I will.
COUNTESS
   It is their lives that stand between our love   130
   That we must smother out, my sovereign.
KING EDWARD
   Whose lives, my lady?
COUNTESS
   Why, my loving liege,
   Your Queen, and Salisbury, my wedded husband,
   Who living own those liens to our love   135

That we cannot exchange but by their death.

KING EDWARD

Your proposition is outside our law.

COUNTESS

So is your desire. If the law

Can bend to execute your carnal will,

Let it bend as you attempt the other.   140

I can't believe you love me as you say

Until you do make good on what you've sworn.

KING EDWARD

No more: your husband and my Queen shall die.

More beautiful than Hero was are you,

But young Leander not as strong as I: 145

He swam an easy current for his love,

But I will through a Hellespont of blood

Immerse myself toward where my Hero waits.

COUNTESS

But you'll do more: you'll stock the river too

With blood from their own two hearts drawn,   150

By whom I mean my husband and your wife.

KING EDWARD

Your beauty makes them guilty of their deaths.

And offers evidence that they should die,

Upon which verdict I as judge condemn them.

COUNTESS *(aside)*

I'm beauty perjured, him corrupted judge!   155

When to the great Star-chamber high above

The Judgment Day calls us to answer for

Our joint-contracted evil, dearly we will pay.

KING EDWARD

What's that, my sweet love? Are you resolved?

COUNTESS

Resolved to be dissolved; and therefore this: 160

Cleave to your word, great King, and I am yours.

Stand where you are. Here's room for you to see —

Mark how I yield my body up to you.

Here by my side have I my wedding knives:

Take you this one, and with it kill your queen,   165

And know by my example where she lies;

And with this other, I'll dispatch my love

Who now lies fast asleep within my heart.

When they are gone, then I'll consent to your —

O dare, lascivious King, to hinder me!   170

My will to die is much more swift, you see,

Than your exertions to prevent it are,

And if you stir again, I die. Be still

And hear the choice that I put forth to you:

Either swear to cease your immoral suit   175

And nevermore solicit sex of me,

Or else, by heaven, with my nuptial knife

I'll smear your floor with that which you would stain,

My poor chaste blood. Swear, Edward, swear,

Or with my death I'll end this foul affair.   180

KING EDWARD

Even with that power that gives me now

The heart to feel the shame in me, I swear.

I hope to never part my lips again

In such a suit that would dishonor you.

Arise, true English lady, we'll exult   185

In you more than the Romans glorified

Lucretia, whose poor plundered body fired

The pens of poets and chroniclers in vain;

Arise, and be my flaw your honor's fame,

Which will enrich you in the days to come. 190
I have awakened from this vexing dream. —
Warwick, my son, Derby, Artois, and Audley,
Brave men of war, where are you all this time?

Enter all

Warwick, I make you Warden of the North.
You, Prince of Wales, and Audley, straight to sea; 195
Meet at Newhaven; some there wait for me.
Myself, Artois, and Derby head through Flanders
To greet our allies there and beg their aid.
This night's too brief for me to take apart
The siege I lay against a lady's heart, 200
For ere the sun engilds the eastern sky,
We'll rouse him with a hearty martial cry.

Exit

ACT 3 ◆ SCENE 1

Enter King John of France, his two sons, Charles of Normandy and
Philip, and the Duke of Lorraine

KING JOHN

    Here, till our navy of a thousand sail

    Have made a breakfast of our foe at sea,

    Let us encamp, and wait for their good word —

    Lorraine, what readiness is Edward in?

    What have you heard, is he well-provisioned   5

    For this his martial exploit on our land?

LORRAINE

    If I may spare you any useless soothing

    And waste your time in idle circumstance,

    It's rumored for a certainty, my lord,

    That he's exceeding strongly fortified;   10

    His subjects flock as willingly to war

    As if to certain triumph they were led.

CHARLES

    England is keen to harbor malcontents,

    Bloodthirsty and seditious Catilines,

    Spendthrifts, and such that gape for nothing else   15

    But tumult and transformation of the state.

    Can such disloyalty engender now

    Loyalty between them?

LORRAINE

    All but David and the Scots who swear,

    As already I have informed his grace,   20

    Never to sheathe their swords or take a truce.

KING JOHN

 Ah, that's an anchor of some better hope.
 Still, on the other hand, to think what allies
 Edward has retained in Netherland,
 Among those ever-bibbing epicures,   25
 Those frothy Dutchmen puffed with double beer,
 That drink and swill in every place they come,
 Does not a little aggravate my spleen.
 What's worse, we hear the Emperor himself
 Endowed him with his own authority.   30
 But all the mightier that the number is,
 The greater glory reaps the victory.
 Some friends have we to gird our native power:
 The obstinate Pole, and the warring Dane,
 The Kings of Bohemia and of Sicily,   35
 Are all declared confederates with us,
 And so I trust this way are marching now.
(drum within)
 But hold, I hear the music of their drums,
 By which I guess that their approach is near.
     Enter the King of Bohemia with Danes,
     and a Polonian captain with other soldiers

KING OF BOHEMIA

 King John of France, as league and vicinity   40
 Require, when friends are any way distressed,
 Expect to see me with my country's force.

POLONIAN CAPTAIN

 And from great Moscow, feared from east to west,
 And lofty Poland, nurse of hardy men,
 These conscripts I do bring to fight for you   45
 Who willingly will venture in your cause.

KING JOHN

Welcome, Bohemian King, and welcome all:
This your great kindness I will not forget.
Beside your plentiful reward in crowns
That from our treasury you will receive,   50
There comes a hare-brained nation, decked in pride,
The spoils of whom will be your triple gain.
And now my hope is full, my joy complete:
At sea we are as potent as the force
Of Agamemnon on the shores of Troy;   55
By land, we're comparable to Xerxes's force,
Whose soldiers drank up rivers in their thirst.
Then reckless, blind, and overweening Ted,
In his mad grab for our royal diadem
Is either to be swallowed with the waves   60
Or hacked to pieces when he comes ashore.

Enter a Mariner

MARINER

Near to the coast I have sighted, my lord,
As I was busy in my watchful charge,
The proud armada of King Edward's ships,
Which, from the distance that I first espied,   65
Seemed, by my view, a grove of withered pines;
But, drawing near, their glorious bright aspect,
Their streaming ensigns wrought of colored silk
Gleamed like a meadow full of sundry flowers
Studding the naked bosom of the earth.   70
Majestical the order of their course,
Mimicking the horned circle of the moon;
And on the top pennant of the flagship,
And likewise all the handmaids of the fleet,
The crests of England and of France conjoined   75

Are quartered equally by herald's art.
Thus, swiftly borne upon a merry gale,
They plow the ocean at full speed for war.

KING JOHN

Does Ted already pluck our fleur-de-lis?
I hope he sucks the honey gathered there   80
And tastes instead the spider's deadly spit
That waits for him upon the poisoned leaves. —
But where's our navy? How are they prepared
To sail themselves against this flight of ravens?

MARINER

They, having knowledge brought them by the scouts,   85
Broke anchor straightaway and puffed with rage,
For that is how I saw their sails with wind.

KING JOHN

There's for your brief. Go back to your vessel;
And if you dodge the bloody stroke of war
And do survive the conflict, come again,   90
And let us know the progress of the fight.

Exit Mariner

Meanwhile, my lords, it's best that we disperse
To separate sites, in case they come ashore.
First you, my lord, with your Bohemian troops,
Shall pitch your battles on the lower marsh;   95
My eldest son, the Duke of Normandy,
Together with this aid of Muscovites,
Shall scale the higher ground another way;
Here in the middle plain, between you both,
Philip, my youngest boy, and I will camp.   100
So, lords, be gone, and look well to your charge:
You stand for France, an empire fair and large.

Exit

Now tell me, Philip, what's your perception
Touching the challenge that the English make?

PHILIP

I say, my Lord, whatever Edward claims —   105
However plain his pedigree appears —
You are the sole possessor of the crown
And that's the surest point of all the law;
But if it weren't, and if he should prevail,
I'll make a conduit of my dearest blood   110
Or chase those straggling upstarts home again.

KING JOHN

Well said, young Philip! Call for bread and wine,
That we may cheer our stomachs with some meal
To look our foes more sternly in the face.

(a table and provisions brought in; the battle heard afar)

Now is begun the heavy day at sea.   115
Fight, Frenchmen, fight; be like the field of bears
When they defend their young cubs in their caves.
Steer, Nemesis, goddess of reprisal
The angry helm, that with your sulph'rous rage
The English fleet may be dispersed and sunk.   120

Cannon shot

PHILIP

O father, how this booming cannon shot
Does harmonize with my cakes' digestion!

KING JOHN

Now, boy, hear what thundering terror 'tis
To buckle for a kingdom's sovereignty!
The earth, with violent trembling when it shakes,   125
Or when the exhalations of a storm
Crack in extremity of lightning flash,
Provokes less fear than kings when they dispose

To show the rancor of their warring hearts.

Enter Mariner

My heart misgives. — O say, pale mariner,   130
To whom belongs the honor of this day.
Relate, I beg you, if your breath allows,
The sad discourse that in your eyes I see.

MARINER

I will, my lord.
My gracious sovereign, France has been repulsed,   135
And boasting Edward triumphs with success.
These hostile iron-hearted navies,
When last I was reporter to your grace,
All full of anger, hope, and fear, and men
Hasting to meet each other hull to hull,   140
At last faced off, and from their flagship
Our flag incurred substantial cannon-shot.
On cue, the others that beheld these ships
Transact a pledge of further ruin,
Like fiery dragons flared ahead in flight,   145
And firing salvoes from their smoky wombs
Sent many grim ambassadors of death.
The sea all crimson, inlets filled as fast
With streaming gore that from the injured spurt
Just as the gushing brine heaved straight into   150
The gaping fissures of the shot-through planks.
Here flew a head dissevered from the trunk,
There mangled arms and legs were tossed aloft,
As when a whirlwind takes the summer dust
And scatters it in middle of the air.   155
Then might you see the reeling vessels split,
And tottering sink into the ruthless deep,
Until their lofty tops were seen no more.

All means were tried, defense and offense both;
And now the consequence of bravery,   160
Of resolution and of cowardice,
Was vividly in play: how one man for fame,
The other by conscription fought and died.
But all in vain. Both sun, the wind, and tide
Defected all to our opponents' side   165
That our force had no choice but to give way,
And they are landed. — Thus my tale is done:
We have untimely lost, and they have won.

KING JOHN

Then nothing left for us except with speed
To join our nations' forces all in one,   170
And bid them fight before they range too far.
Come, gentle Philip, let's from here depart.
This sailor's words have cleft your father's heart.

Exit

ACT 3 ♦ SCENE 2

Enter two Frenchmen;
a woman and two little children meet them and other citizens

ONE

Well met, my brethren. Come now, what's the news,
And why are you so laden up with stuff?
What, is it moving day that makes you trek
With heavy bag and baggage too?

TWO

Moving day? More like head-removing day!   5
Have you not heard the news that bruits about?

ONE

What news?

TWO

How the French navy is destroyed at sea,
And that the English army has arrived.

ONE

Calm down, man; they are far enough from here   10
And will be met, I promise you, to their loss
If they do break so far into the realm.

TWO

Right, as the grasshopper idles his days
In mirth and jollity till winter comes,
And then too late! He can't buy back the time,   15
When frozen cold has nipped his careless head.
We're charged to lead this train of refugees
And will prepare in time for their relief
Lest when we need it most, there's none to find.

ONE

It seems to me you're counting on defeat   20
And hope your country will be overthrown.

THREE

We only know it's good to fear the worst.

ONE

Then fight like men, not run like craven boys
Abandoning their parents in distress!

TWO

Tush, those that have already taken arms   25
Are millions and formidable, compared
To those small factions of our enemies.
And yet the quarrel's hard to quarrel with:
This Edward is our late king's sister's son.
While John of Valois's three degrees removed.   30

WOMAN

Besides, there comes a prophecy to mind,
Published by one that was a friar once,
Whose oracles have often proven true;
In it he says, the time will shortly come
When roused, a wrathful lion from the west 35
Shall carry off the fleur-de-lis of France.
This and other portents, let me tell you,
Are shafts of ice in many Gallic hearts.

Enter a Frenchman

FRENCHMAN

Run, countrymen and citizens of France!
Sweet flow'ring peace, the root of happy life, 40
Abandoned by the realm, abandons us;
As far off as these mortal eyes could see
I thought I saw five cities all on fire,
Cornfields and vineyards burning like an oven;
And as the wind took on the rising smoke 45
And then dispersed it from my view, I saw
The dwellers running from their flaming homes
To fall in droves upon the soldiers' pikes.
Here on the right hand comes the conquering King,
And on the left his hot unbridled son, 50
And in between, our nation's gleaming troops;
All which, though separate, yet converge as one
To leave a desolation where they come.
And therefore, citizens, I urge you go!
Seek out some safer refuge further off. 55

Exit

ACT 3 ◆ SCENE 3

Enter King Edward and the Earl of Derby with soldiers
and Gobin de Grace

KING EDWARD

Where's the Frenchman who cunningly for us
Revealed the shallows of this River Somme
And through the estuary led our ships?

GOBIN

Here, my good lord.

KING EDWARD

What are you called? Tell me your name.   5

GOBIN

Gobin de Grace, if please your excellence.

KING EDWARD

Then, Gobin, for the service you have done,
We here endow you with your liberty;
And, for recompense beside this gift,
You will receive five hundred marks in gold. —   10
I know not how we should have found our way
To Ned, for whom my heart now longs to see.

Enter Artois

ARTOIS

Good news, my lord; the Prince approaches fast,
And with him comes Lord Audley and the rest,
Whom since our landing we have urged to join.   15

Enter Prince Edward, Lord Audley, and soldiers

KING EDWARD

Welcome, brave Prince! How have you fared, my son,
Since your arrival on the coast of France?

PRINCE EDWARD

Successfully, I thank the gracious heavens.
Some of their strongest cities we have won

And others we have wasted utterly   20
For no one to progress and live upon.
Those who conceded we kindly pardoned,
While those refusers of our proffered peace
Incurred the penalty of sharp revenge.

KING EDWARD

Ah, France, why must you be so obstinate   25
Against the kind embraces of your friends?
How gently had we thought to stir your heart
And set our foot upon your tender clay;
Instead, in willful and disdainful pride
You, like a skittish and unbroken colt,   30
Would buck and stamp, and strike your hooves on us!
But tell me, Ned, throughout your war campaign
Have you not seen the usurper King of France?

PRINCE EDWARD

Yes, my good lord, and not two hours ago,
But with a hundred thousand fighting men   35
Upon the one side of the river's bank,
And on the other, all his allies too.
No doubt he would have crushed our smaller force;
But luckily, perceiving your approach,
He has withdrawn his troops to Crécy plains,   40
Where judging by deployment of his men,
He means to challenge us in battle soon.

KING EDWARD

He shall be welcome; that's the thing we crave.

Enter King John, Dukes of Normandy and Lorraine,
King of Bohemia, young Philip, and soldiers

KING JOHN

Edward, know that John, the true King of France,
Appalled by your invasion of his land   45

47

And by your tyrannous propensity
To slay his subjects and subdue his towns,
Spits in your face; and in these ensuing terms
Indicts you for this arrogant incursion:
First, I condemn you for a miscreant, 50
A pirate, deficient in all senses,
One that has either no abiding home,
Or else, inhabiting some barren soil
Where neither herb nor fruitful grain can grow,
Survives entirely by pilfering; 55
Next, insofar as you have broken faith
And league and solemn covenant made with me,
I take you for a lying craven wretch;
And, last of all, although I scorn to cope
With someone so inferior to myself, 60
Yet, as it seems your thirst is all for gold,
Preferring rather to be feared than loved,
Then here am I to satisfy your wish
In either case, for with me have I brought
A royal store of treasure, pearl, and coin. 65
Thus cease your persecution of the weak
And taste some conflict armed against the armed.
Forget your other petty thefts; let's see
You try to win this pillage manfully.

KING EDWARD

If bile or wormwood have a pleasant taste, 70
Then is your salutation honey-sweet;
But since their flavor is all bitterness,
So bitterly do we your words receive.
Yet here's how I regard your worthless taunts:
If you have uttered them to dim my fame 75
Or taint the reputation of my birth,

Know that your wolfish tongue does wag in vain;
Consider, Valois, whether I intend
To skirmish not for plunder, but for the crown
That's on your head, and that I vow to have,   80
As one of us is bound to gravely feel.

PRINCE EDWARD

One thing more, briefly, may I, Father, please:
Since shamelessly your throat is varnished
With scandalous and most notorious lies,
While our contended cause is truly just,   85
So let our battle end this way today:
May you or us prevail and win the field
Or, luckless, cursed, endure eternal shame!

KING EDWARD

There's nothing more to add to that; I know
His conscience clearly sees what is my right.   90
Therefore Valois, say, will you abdicate,
Before the sickle's thrust into the corn
Or our enkindled fury turns to flame?

KING JOHN

Edward, I know what right brings you to France
But I say that before I yield the crown   95
This champion field will be a pool of blood
And turn our prospects to a slaughterhouse.

PRINCE EDWARD

Ay, that confirms the tyrant that you are:
No father, king, or shepherd of the realm,
But one that would his kingdom tear apart   100
And like a tiger suck the entrails out.

AUDLEY

You peers of France, why do you follow him
That would so prodigally misuse your lives?

49

CHARLES

 Whom should we follow, doddering old fool,

 But he that is our true-born sovereign?   105

KING EDWARD

 You reprimand this man because his face

 By Time has marks of age engraved on it?

 Take heed, these grave scholars of experience,

 Like stiff-grown oaks, will stand immovable

 When whirlwinds quickly turn up younger trees.   110

DERBY

 Did any of your forebears ever rule

 As King except yourself before this day?

 Edward's great lineage, on his mother's side,

 Five hundred years has held the scepter up.

 Judge then, conspirators, by his descent,   115

 Who is the true-born sovereign: he or that.

PHILIP

 Father, plan our tactics, prate no more.

 These English gladly waste the day with words

 Until nightfall, when they'll slip away unfought.

KING JOHN

 Lords and my loving subjects, now's the time   120

 That your assembled force must bear the test.

 Therefore, my friends, consider this my brief:

 He that you fight for is your natural king,

 He that you fight against a foreigner,

 He that you fight for rules with tolerance   125

 And reins you with a mild and gentle bit;

 He that you fight against, if he succeeds,

 Will promptly crown himself in tyranny,

 Make slaves of you, and with a heavy hand

 Curtail and curb your sweetest liberty.   130

So, to protect your country and your king,
Let all the lusty courage of your hearts
Match with the power of your able hands,
And watch how quick these renegades will run.
For what's this Edward but a *bon vivant*,   135
A tenderhearted womanizing rake,
That I heard almost killed himself for love?
And what, I ask you, is his royal guard?
This lot, which if you take away their beef
And repossess their downy featherbeds,   140
You'll find them all as stiff and spiritless
As teams of sway-backed overridden nags.
So, Frenchmen, scorn that these should be your lords,
But rather shackle them for thinking so.

ALL FRENCHMEN
    Vive le roi! God save King John of France!   145

KING JOHN
    Now on this plain of Crécy spread yourselves —
    And, Edward, when you dare, begin the charge.
                    Exit King John and Frenchmen

KING EDWARD
    We will engage you shortly, John of France. —
    Now, English lords, let us resolve this day
    To either clear these charges from ourselves   150
    Or else die trying for our innocence.
    And, Ned, because this battle is the first
    Upon a pitchèd field you've ever fought,
    The old knight-errant code obliges us
    To mark you with the crest of chivalry   155
    And solemnly bestow your arms on you.
    Come, therefore, heralds, formally bring on
    The proper garments for the Prince my son.

Enter four heralds bringing in a coat armor,
a helmet, a lance, and a shield

Edward Plantagenet, in the name of God,
As with this armor I enfold your breast,   160
So may your noble unrelenting heart
Be cased with flint and matchless fortitude,
That base affections never may intrude.
Fight and be valiant, conquer where you tread! —
Now follow, lords, and do him honor too.   165
DERBY

Edward Plantagenet, Prince of Wales,
As I do set this helmet on your head,
Where within lies the chamber of your brain,
So may your temples by the gods of war
Be crowned with laurel victory this day.   170
Fight and be valiant, conquer where you tread!
AUDLEY

Edward Plantagenet, Prince of Wales,
Receive this lance into your manly hand
And use it as you would a brazen pen
To draw forth bloody stratagems in France   175
And print your valiant deeds in honor's book.
Fight and be valiant, conquer where you tread!
KING EDWARD

All that remains is knighthood, which deferred
We leave till you have earned it in the field.
PRINCE EDWARD

My gracious father, and you, ranking peers,   180
This honor you do me invigorates
And thrills my green but enripening strength
With reassuring and auspicious signs.
If ever I profane these hallowed gifts

Or fail to use them for the good of God,   185
The sake of all the fatherless and poor,
And for the benefit of England's peace,
Then freeze, my joints, turn feeble, arms of mine,
Wither, my heart, till like a sapless tree
I'll stand for shame in my deformity.   190

KING EDWARD

Then thus our formations will be fixed:
The leading of the vanguard, Ned, is yours,
But I will temper your vitality
By pairing it with Audley's gravity
So that courage with experience joined   195
Will make your execution consummate.
The chief battalion, I will guide myself
With Derby in the rearward march behind.
All this deployed in militant array,
Let's ride to war, and God grant us the day!   200

Exit

ACT 3 ♦ SCENE 4

Alarum. Enter many fleeing Frenchmen. After them Prince Edward
running. Then enter King John and Duke of Lorraine.

KING JOHN

Oh, Lorraine, speak, why do our men run?
We far outnumber all our meager foes.

LORRAINE

The garrison soldiers of Genoese
That came from Paris worn out by their march
Grudging to be so instantly deployed,   5
No sooner at the front took up their place
Than, falling back, so dismayed the rest
That every unit scattered in retreat,

Which in their haste to make a safe escape,
A thousandfold and more were crushed to death   10
Than ever by the enemy were slain.

KING JOHN

Unfortunate wretches! Still, let's assay
To keep their spirits up and make them stay!

Exit

ACT 3 ♦ SCENE 5

Enter King Edward and Audley

KING EDWARD

Lord Audley, while our son goes in pursuit,
Encamp our men upon this hillock here,
And let us breathe ourselves a season's rest.

AUDLEY

I will, my lord.

Exit. Sound retreat.

KING EDWARD

Merciful heaven, whose secret providence   5
To our dim judgment is inscrutable,
How bound we are to praise your wondrous will,
That deemed it fit to give this day to us,
And made the wicked stumble in their cause.

Enter Artois

ARTOIS

A rescue, King, a rescue for your son!   10

KING EDWARD

Rescue, Artois? What, is he prisoner,
Or by some violence stricken from his horse?

ARTOIS

Neither, my lord; but desperately besieged
By the rallying French he was pursuing;

54

His certain doom approaches even now   15
Unless your highness will deliver him!

KING EDWARD

Tut, let him fight; we armed him well today,
Besides, he's working on his knighthood, man.

Enter Derby

DERBY

The Prince, my Lord, the Prince! He must be saved!
A world of turmoil has engirdled him!   20

KING EDWARD

Then he will earn a world of honor too
If he by valor can redeem himself.
If not, it's what it is; we have more sons
Than one to comfort our declining years.

Enter Audley

AUDLEY

O honored Edward, please let me command   25
My soldiers to deliver safe your son,
For I'm afraid these hazards will dispatch him.
The French maneuvers, like swarms of fire ants,
Bristle about him; while like a lion
Entangled in the net of their assaults,   30
He madly rends and roars on every side
But vainly since he cannot free himself.

KING EDWARD

Audley, at ease. No, not a single man,
On pain of death, will after Ned be sent.
This day's the day, ordained by destiny,   35
That seasons his courage with mortal thoughts
And if he lives he'll savor when he's old
The exploit that defined his gilded days.

DERBY

    That's if he ever lives to see those days.

KING EDWARD

    Well, then his epitaph is lasting praise.   40

AUDLEY

    And yet, my lord, your willfulness exceeds

    The need to shed his blood so wantonly.

KING EDWARD

    Enough of this! For none of you can tell

    If rescue will do any good at all.

    He could be dead or taken prisoner;   45

    Distract a falcon while she's in midflight

    And never will her hunting be as right;

    Pluck Edward from the dangers of this world

    And ever after he'll expect the same;

    But if by himself he redeems himself,   50

    He'll vanquish death and fear and doubtfulness.

    And blithely so regard their force no more

    Than if they were mere babes or captive slaves.

AUDLEY

    O cruel father! Farewell Edward, then.

ARTOIS

    Oh, that my life would ransom his from death!   55

KING EDWARD

    But hold, it seems I hear

    The dismal blare of the trumpeter's retreat.

    They're not all dead, I hope, that went with him;

    Some will return with news both good or bad.

    Enter Prince Edward in triumph, bearing in his hand his splintered

    lance, with the body of the King of Bohemia borne before, wrapped

    in his flag. They run and embrace him.

AUDLEY

O joyous sight, triumphant Edward lives!   60

DERBY

Welcome, brave Prince!

KING EDWARD

Welcome, Plantagenet!

The Prince kneels and kisses his father's hand

PRINCE EDWARD

First, good my lords, as duty does oblige,

Let me salute you all with hearty thanks.

And here with humble duty I present   65

This sacrifice, this first fruit of my sword

Cropped and cut down even at the gate of death:

Bohemia's King, my father, by me slain,

Whose legions had entrenched me round about

And thrashed as hard upon my battered shield   70

As on an anvil with their weighty spears.

I did directly call to mind these gifts

You gave me with the fervent vow I swore,

And then new courage freshened me again.

See thus how Edward's hand fulfilled your will   75

And done, I hope the duty of a knight.

His sword borne by a soldier

KING EDWARD

Ay, well you've earned a proper knighthood, Ned;

And therefore with your sword, still reeking warm

With blood of those who strove to bring you down,

Arise, Prince Edward, trusty knight at arms.   80

This day you have confounded me with joy,

And proved yourself a fit heir for a king.

PRINCE EDWARD

A tally here, my gracious lord, of those

Our foes that in this battle have been slain:
Eleven princes of esteem, fourscore barons,   85
A hundred and twenty knights, and thirty thousand
Common soldiers; and on our side, a thousand.

KING EDWARD

Our God be praised! Now, John of France, you know
King Edward for no womanizing rake,
No love-sick cockney, nor his soldiers' nags.   90
But which way has our timid king escaped?

PRINCE EDWARD

Towards Poitiers, noble father, with his sons.

KING EDWARD

Ned, you and Audley stay on their pursuit;
Myself and Derby to Calais will go
And bid our men that seaside town lay siege.   95
It all depends upon this final stroke,
So strike with vigor while the game's afoot, —
What picture's this?

PRINCE EDWARD

A pelican, my lord,
Gashing her bosom with her crooked beak,   100
So that her nest of young ones might be fed
With drops of blood that issue from her heart:
The motto *Sic et vos*: "and so should you."

Exit

ACT 4 ◆ SCENE 1

Enter Lord Mountford, a coronet in his hand,
with the Earl of Salisbury

MOUNTFORD

My lord of Salisbury, since with your help
My enemy, Sir Charles of Blois, is dead,
And I again have duly repossessed
My Brittany dukedom, know that I resolve,
For this kind service of your king and you,   5
To swear allegiance to his majesty:
For token which I give this coronet.
Offer it to him, together with my oath
To always stand as Edward's faithful friend.

SALISBURY

I'll bear it, Mountford. But I hope by then   10
The whole dominion of the realm of France
Will be surrendered to his conquering hand.

Exit Mountford

Now, if I had some way to safely pass,
I would at Calais gladly meet his grace,
Where I go since these letters certify   15
That he intends to pull his armies back.
This policy dictates it: I must go. —
Guards, who's within? — Bring Villiers to me.

Enter Villiers

Villiers, you know that as my prisoner,
I might for ransom, if I choose to do,   20
Reprieve you for a hundred thousand francs,
Or else retain and keep you captive still.

59

But as it happens, for a smaller charge
You may acquit yourself, if you're so disposed.
And this it is: procure for me a passport   25
From Charles, Duke of Normandy, so that
Without restraint I may access Calais
Through all the countries where he has some sway,
Which you should easily obtain, I think,
Since after all I've often heard you say   30
He and you were students once together;
Perform this and you'll have your liberty.
What's your thought? Will you undertake to do it?

VILLIERS

I will, my lord, but I must speak with him.

SALISBURY

Well then, go mount your horse and hasten there! —   35
Only before you go, swear on your faith
That if you fail to carry out my wish
You will return as prisoner again
And that will be sufficient warrant for me.

VILLIERS

To this condition, I do swear, my lord,   40
And will most earnestly perform my charge.

Exit

SALISBURY

Farewell Villiers.
We'll see how well a Frenchman keeps his word.

Exit

ACT 4 ◆ SCENE 2

Enter King Edward and Derby with soldiers

KING EDWARD

Since they refuse our terms of peace, my lord,

And put up barricades against us,
We will entrench our men on every side,
That neither reinforcements nor supplies
May bring relief to this abysmal town.   5
Where swords may falter, famine will prevail.

Enter six poor Frenchmen

DERBY

The promised aid that made them resolute
Never appeared but went another way:
'Twill surely purge them of their stubborn will. —
But what are these poor ragged strays, my lord?   10

KING EDWARD

Ask who they are; it seems they come from Calais.

DERBY

You specimens of wretchedness and woe,
What are you, living men or gliding ghosts
Arisen from your graves to walk the earth?

A POOR FRENCHMAN

No ghosts my lord but men that breathe a life   15
Far worse than is the quiet sleep of death.
We are Calais's beleaguered citizens,
The most diseased, malformed, and starved of us
And now because we are not fit to serve,
The captain of the town has cast us out   20
So that provisions may be spared.

KING EDWARD

Such charity, and so laudable too!
But what do you imagine happens now?
We are your enemies; the rules of war
Require no less than you be put to death   25
Since when we proffered truce, it was refused.

61

POOR FRENCHMAN

Then if your grace won't supersede such rules,

We welcome death as willingly as life.

KING EDWARD

Poor men, so wronged, and needlessly besides!

Go, Derby, go and see to their relief.   30

Command that food and water be provided,

And give to each of them five crowns apiece.

Exit Derby and Frenchmen

The lion scorns to touch the yielding prey,

Yet Edward's sword will sheathe itself in flesh

Of those who brought on this barbarity.   35

Enter Lord Percy

Lord Percy, welcome. What's the news in England?

PERCY

The Queen, my lord, sends greetings to your grace,

And from her highness and the lord vice-regent

I bring this fresh and happy word of home:

David of Scotland, armed for war again,   40

Presumably believing he'd prevail

Without your highness to defend the realm

Is, by the stalwart service of your peers

And painful labors of the Queen herself,

Who, big with child, fought off the Scots herself,   45

Vanquished, subdued, and taken prisoner.

KING EDWARD

Thanks, Percy, for this news, with all my heart!

Who was it took him captive in the field?

PERCY

A squire, my Lord; John Copeland is his name,

Who, shunning all her majesty's appeals   50

Refuses to relinquish his prize catch

To anyone except your grace alone,

Which grievously displeases our Queen.

KING EDWARD

Well, then we'll have a messenger dispatched

To summon Copeland promptly to our sight   55

Accompanied by his prisoner king.

PERCY

My lord, the Queen's herself at sea by now

And hopes, as soon as wind will serve her course,

To harbor at Calais and visit you.

KING EDWARD

I welcome her approach, and to that end   60

I'll pitch my tent near by the sandy shore.

Enter a French captain

CAPTAIN

The burghers of Calais, your majesty,

Have by a council willingly decreed

To yield the town and castle to your hands,

Upon condition that it please your grace   65

To furnish them with goods and spare their lives.

KING EDWARD

Is that so? Then apparently they call,

Decree, elect, and govern as they please!

No, Captain, tell them, since they first refused

The generous clemency that I proclaimed   70

They will not have it now, as it's revoked.

I mandate nothing less than fire and sword

Unless, within these two days, six of them

That are the wealthiest merchants in the town

Come naked, clad in only linen shirts,   75

With hangman's nooses tied around each neck

And yield themselves outstretched upon their knees

To be abused or hanged or what I please;
Inform their lordships of my kind reply.

Exit Edward and Percy

CAPTAIN

This comes from trusting promises unkept.   80
Had we not been advised that John our King
Would march his army straight to our defense,
We might have sooner opened wide our gates.
But what's befallen now we can't recall,
And some may perish for the sake of all.   85

Exit

ACT 4 ◆ SCENE 3

Enter Charles of Normandy and Villiers

CHARLES

I marvel, Villiers, that you beg of me
Support for one I count my enemy.

VILLIERS

Not merely for his sake, my gracious lord,
Do I become his earnest advocate,
But so that I may earn my ransom off.   5

CHARLES

Your ransom? Man, what good is ransom now?
Are you not free? And don't we prize the times
That work against the good of all our foes
As something to be sought and lauded for?

VILLIERS

No, good my lord, unless it's justified;   10
Since profit must with honor be infused
Or else our actions are unprincipled.
But notwithstanding your objections, sire,
Will you subscribe to his request or not?

CHARLES

    Villiers, I cannot do it nor shall I.   15

    Salisbury will not have his way with me

    To claim a passport just to please himself.

VILLIERS

    Why then I know the consequence, my lord.

    I must return to prison as agreed.

CHARLES

    Return? I hope you won't.   20

    What bird that has escaped the fowler's trap

    Will not beware how she's ensnared again?

VILLIERS

    But it's the pledge I made, my gracious lord

    Which I in conscience may not overstep

    Even if my kingdom should command it.   25

CHARLES

    Your pledge? Why, that's what binds you here with us!

    Have you not sworn obedience to your prince?

VILLIERS

    In all things that you prudently command,

    But if you should persuade or threaten me

    Not to obey the covenant of my word,   30

    That's criminal and duty ceases there.

CHARLES

    How is it legal for a man to kill

    And not to break a promise with his foe?

VILLIERS

    To kill, my lord, when parties are at war

    To right the wrongs perceived by each of them   35

    No doubt is lawfully permitted us,

    But in an oath we must be well advised

    What we swear to and for and what it means

Not to infringe on it on pain of death.
And so, I willingly return, my lord, 40
As if my soul were bound to paradise.

CHARLES

Stay, my Villiers, your honorable mind
Deserves to be eternally revered.
Your suit will be no longer thus deferred.
Give me the paper, I'll sign it now 45
And where before I loved you as Villiers,
Hereafter I'll embrace you as myself.
Stay, you remain in favor with our realm.

VILLIERS

I humbly thank your grace, I must press on
And first remit this passport to the earl 50
After which I serve your highness's pleasure.

CHARLES

Do so;

Exit Villiers

And if by chance my ranks grow thin
I pray for soldiers half as good as him.

Enter King John

KING JOHN

Come Charles, and armor up! We have Edward trapped! 55
The Prince of Wales has erred into our zone
And we've surrounded him, he can't escape!

CHARLES

But will your highness fight today?

KING JOHN

What else? He marches with eight thousand men,
While we are sixty thousand strong at least. 60

CHARLES

I have a prophecy, my gracious lord,

Wherein is written what the likely end
Will be for us in this appalling war.
It was relayed to me at Crécy field
By some decrepit hermit living there.
(reads)
"When feathered fowl shall make your army tremble,   65
And flint rocks rise and break the battleline,
Then think on him that does not now dissemble,
For that shall be the fateful dreaded sign.
Yet in the end you'll set your foot as far
In England as your foe will set in France."   70

KING JOHN

By this I gauge that luck is with our troops:
For, since it is impossible that stones
Should ever rise and break the battlelines,
Or hov'ring birds cause hardened men to quake,
It's likely that we're on the winning side.   75
Supposing that it's true, though; in the end,
Since he portends that we shall drive them out
And plunder their land as they plundered ours,
The loss with this revenge won't be as harsh.
Anyway, it's whims and fancies, toys and dreams: 80
Once we've laid the trap for Edward's son,
Then Edward father will be set upon.

Exit

ACT 4 ◆ SCENE 4

Enter Prince Edward, Audley, and others

PRINCE EDWARD

Audley, I feel the arms of death's embrace,
And comfort have we none, save that to die
We pay sour interest for a sweeter life.

At Crécy Field our warsmoke clouded up
And choked those Frenchmen's mouths and scattered them;   5
But now their multitudes of millions teem,
Eclipsing all the beauteous burning sun,
Leaving us no hope but the sullen dark
And dreadful blindness of world-ending night.

AUDLEY

This sudden, mighty, and ingenious surge   10
That they have made, fair prince, is staggering.
Before us in the valley waits the king,
Supplied with all that God and earth can yield,
His fierce battalions larger than our own.
His son, the braying Duke of Normandy,   15
Has decked the mountain on our right in plates
Of shining armor that now the rising hills
Gleam like a silver quarry, or a crown,
While over them the banners, bannerets,
And undulating pennants cuff the air   20
And beat the winds that insolently try
To kiss their splendor. On our left hand lies
Philip, the younger scion of the king,
Crowding the other hill in such array
That all his gilded upright pikes appear   25
As trees of gold, with blazonry for leaves;
Behind, this mountain does impose its height
For, like a half-moon opening but one way,
It hems us in: there at the rear are lodged
The fatal crossbows, which battalion is   30
Commanded by the rough Chattillion.
And so it stands: the valley for our flight
The king binds in; the hills on either side
Are occupied by his majestic sons;

And on the mount behind stands certain death   35
Paid for and serviced by Chattillion.
PRINCE EDWARD
Death is more than the sum of all the dead:
This parceling of powers enlarges them
To fill the world and yet it's still one power.
There is but one France, one king of France: 40
This single nation with a single king
Has but a single army of one king,
And we are one as well. Then fear no odds,
For one against one is equal and fair.
                    Enter Herald 1 from King John
What's the word, messenger? Be plain and brief.   45
HERALD
The King of France, my sovereign lord and master,
Greets you the Prince of Wales, his foe, through me.
If you call forth a hundred of your peers,
Your lords, knights, squires, and English gentlemen,
And with yourself and them kneel at his feet,   50
He will directly fold his bloody colors up
And pay his ransom for lives forfeited;
If not, this day shall drink more English blood
Than ever spilled upon our Breton earth.
What is your answer to this proffered mercy?   55
PRINCE EDWARD
My tongue is made of steel and it will beg
My mercy on his coward coronet.
Tell him my colors are as red as his,
My men as bold, our English arms as strong.
Return him my defiance to his face.   60
HERALD
I go.

Exit Herald 1; enter Herald 2

PRINCE EDWARD

And what of you?

HERALD

The Duke of Normandy, my lord and master,

In pity of your youth in this distress,

Had me bring a nimble-jointed pony 65

As swift as any you put saddle on,

And on that gift he urges you to leave

Or death himself shall cut you where you breathe.

PRINCE EDWARD

Back with the beast to the beast that sent him!

Tell him I will not ride a coward's horse 70

But he should ride the nag away himself,

For I will stain my horse's shanks with blood

And double drench my spurs, but I will catch him.

Go tell the mincing boy this and begone!

Exit Herald 2; enter Herald 3

HERALD

Edward of Wales, Philip the second son 75

Of the most mighty Christian King of France,

Seeing your body's living date expired,

With Christian love and pious charity

Bestows this holy book inscribed with prayers

To your good care, and for your final hour 80

Beseeches you to find the peace therein

And brace your soul for its long journey home.

Thus have I done his bidding and return.

PRINCE EDWARD

Herald, send your lord this word from me:

All good that he can spare, I will receive, 85

But don't you think the ill-considered boy

Has wronged himself by giving this to me?
Perhaps he cannot pray without the book:
He is, I think, no practiced reverend.
Then let him take his common psalter back 90
To do him good in his adversity.
Besides, what does he know about my sins
And how can he presume to pray for them?
Before night falls, his prayer to God may be
That I will hear his prayers to spare his life. 95
So tell the courtly rogue this, I pray you.

HERALD

I will.

Exit

PRINCE

How confident their strength of numbers makes them!
Now, Audley, beat your wings of silvered hair
And let those thin white messengers of time 100
Impart their learning in this fatal hour.

AUDLEY

To die is all as common as to live:
While one's a choice, the other is a chase
Since, from the instant we begin to live
We do pursue and hunt the time of death. 105
We bud and then we bloom, then sow our seed,
And shortly after, wilt; and as a shade
Follows the body, so we follow death.
If then we hunt for death, why do we fear it?
If we fear it, why do we follow it? 110
For, whether ripe or rotten, drop we shall,
As destined by the lottery of our days.

PRINCE EDWARD

Ah, good old man, these words of yours are all

71

The armor I need plated on my back.
Ah, Life, how foolish you seem when we seek   115
The thing you fear, and how diminished Death
Becomes in murderous victory over us
When all the lives his slaying arrows seek
Have sought out him and thereby dimmed his glory.
I will not give a penny for my life   120
Nor half of that to shun my bleakest death,
Since now to live is but to seek to die
And dying the beginning of new life.
The hour is come and it is mine to rule.
To live or die means nothing to this fool.   125

Exit

ACT 4 ◆ SCENE 5

Enter King John and Charles

KING JOHN

A sudden darkness has defaced the sky,
The winds are crept into their caves for fear,
The leaves move not, the world is hushed and still,
The birds cease singing and the wand'ring brooks
Withdraw their murmured greeting to their shores.   5
Silence awaits some wonder, as if sensing
That heaven should pronounce some prophecy.
Where or from whom proceeds this silence, Charles?
CHARLES

Our men, with mouths agape and staring eyes,
Look on each other, as they wait to hear   10
Each other's words, and yet no words are voiced.
A dumbstruck fear has midnight made of day,
And speech is deadened in all waking regions.

KING JOHN

    Before, the brilliant sun in all his pride

    Looked through his golden coach upon the world,

    But now impulsively has hid his face   15

    And turned the earth below into a grave,

    Dark, deadly, silent, and discomfiting.

(a clamor of ravens)

    God, what a deadly outcry do I hear?

CHARLES

    Here comes my brother Philip.

PHILIP

    A flight, a flight!   20

KING JOHN

    Coward, what flight? Lies, I called no retreat.

PHILIP

    A flight!

KING JOHN

    Rouse up your craven heart and relay

    To us the source and substance of that fear

    Which is so ghastly printed on your face.   25

PHILIP

    A flight of ugly ravens

    Do croak and hover over our brigade

    And keep their squadrons in formation

    While for the battle we prepare below.

    With their approach there came this sudden fog,   30

    Which hid from us the fiery flower of heaven

    And made at noon a night unnatural

    Upon the quaking and astonished world.

    In brief, our soldiers have their weapons dropped

    And stand like statues metamorphosed there,   35

    Bloodless and pale, eyes on each other fixed.

KING JOHN *(aside)*

Ah, now there comes the prophecy on cue
But I must bolt my door against this fear. —
Return, and reassure these gullibles:
Tell them the ravens, seeing them armed,   40
So many fair against a famished few,
Come but to dine upon their handiwork
And prey upon the carrion that they kill.
Like when we see a dying horse collapse,
Although not dead, the ravenous birds   45
Sit watching the departure of his life,
Even so these ravens, for the carcasses
Of those poor English that are marked to die,
Hover about, and if they cry and caw
It's for the meat that we must kill for them.   50
I must away and hearten up my soldiers
And sound the trumpets to dispel at once
This little business of a silly fraud.

Exit Prince

Another noise. Salisbury brought in by a French captain.

CAPTAIN

Behold, my liege, this knight and forty more,
Of whom the better part are slain or fled,   55
Tried every way and more to break our ranks
To lend his aid to the surrounded prince.
Dispose of him as please your majesty.

KING JOHN

Go, and the next limb, soldier, that you find,
Disgrace it with his body straight away;   60
For I do hold a tree in France too good
To be the gallows of an English thief.

SALISBURY

    My Lord of Normandy, I have your pass

    And warrant for my safety through this land.

CHARLES

    Villiers procured it for you, did he not?   65

SALISBURY

    He did.

CHARLES

    And it is valid: you may freely pass.

KING JOHN

    Ay, freely to the gallows to be hanged

    Away with him!

CHARLES

    I hope your highness won't embarrass me   70

    And flout the honor of my noble crest.

    He has my reputable name to show,

    Signed and sealed with this royal hand of mine;

    I rather would disown my life as prince

    Than disavow the pledge I made as prince.   75

    I do beseech you, let him pass in peace.

KING JOHN

    Your word and you fall under my command.

    What can you promise that I cannot break?

    Which of these two brings you the most disgrace,

    To disobey your father or yourself?   80

    Your word, nor any man's, should not exceed

    My power to break it, nor should you ever

    Infringe upon your utmost word to me.

    The breach of faith presumes the soul's consent,

    Which, if you're forced without consent to break,   85

    Then you are not to blame for breach of faith.

    Go, hang him: for your word is mine to give

And when I deign to break it, you'll forgive.
CHARLES
Did I not swear to be a soldier too?
Then arms adieu and let the war be damned. 90
Should I not tear the swordbelt from my waist,
Or do I need a guardian to control
Precisely when I give my things away?
Upon my soul, had Edward Prince of Wales
Consigned his word, penned in his noble hand, 95
To let your knights pass through his father's land,
The royal king in favor to his son
Would not safe-conduct only give to them,
But grant them bounteous feast along the way.
KING JOHN
Prefer you their example? Very well. 100
Tell me, English, the rank among your peers.
SALISBURY
An earl in England, though a prisoner here,
And those that know me call me Salisbury.
KING JOHN
Then, Salisbury, say to whom you go and where.
SALISBURY
To Calais, where my liege King Edward is. 105
KING JOHN
To Calais, Salisbury? Then to Calais crawl,
And bid your king to dig a noble grave
To put his brazen son, black Edward, in.
And as you travel westward from this place
Some two leagues on, you'll see a lofty hill 110
Whose top seems topless, for embracing sky
Conceals its head within her azure bosom.
And when you're safely there upon that crest

Look down toward the humble vale below,
Once barren but now proudly decked with arms,   115
And there descry the wretched Prince of Wales
All manacled and shackled round about.
Then to Calais carry on as I have willed
And say the prince was kenneled and not killed;
But tell your Edward this is not the worst,   120
For sooner than he thinks, I'll meet him first.
Away; and if our bullets find you not,
Then choke on smoke that from their guns are shot.

Exit

ACT 4 ◆ SCENE 6

Alarum. Enter Prince Edward and Artois.

ARTOIS

How fares your grace? Have you been shot my lord?

PRINCE EDWARD

No, dear Artois, but choked with dust and smoke,
I gasp aside for breath and fresher air.

ARTOIS

Breathe then and back again, the French are stunned
And full engrossed with gazing on the crows   5
And if our quivers weren't devoid of shafts
Your grace would see such glory on this day!
O arrows, Lord, we want more arrows still!

PRINCE EDWARD

Courage, Artois, who needs the feathered shafts
When we have feathered allies on our side.   10
Look, look, Artois, the ground itself is armed
With fire-starting flint, direct our men
To set their pretty-colored longbows by
And hurl these stones instead. Away, Artois, away

My soul predicts we will command the day!

Exit

ACT 4 ◆ SCENE 7

Alarum. Enter King John.

KING JOHN

Our legions are in themselves confounded,
Appalled, distraught, while a viral panic
Has roused a cold dismay through all our ranks,
And every petty disadvantage spurs
The dread-infected abject soul to flee.   5
Even I, whose spirit is steel to their dull lead,
Recalling the vile prophecy of birds
And how our native flint from English arms
Rebelled against us, find myself stricken
With most surprising and unyielding fear.   10

Enter Charles

CHARLES

Go, father, run! The French are killing French,
They're cutting down defectors in retreat;
Our drums strike nothing but discouragement;
Our trumpets sound dishonor and fade off;
The spirit of fear that fears only death   15
Is working its confusion on itself!

Enter Philip

PHILIP

Pluck out your eyes or you'll see this day's shame!
Some handful naked scarecrows with small flints
Have driven back a mighty host of men
Arrayed in all their military trappings.   20

KING JOHN

God's death! We're just a children's game to them!

No less than forty thousand hardy warriors
Are stoned to death this day by forty rogues!

CHARLES

O let me be some other countryman!
This day has set derision on the French,   25
And all the world will blurt their scorn at us.

KING JOHN

Unite those still about. The scant percent
Of us who live are men enough to push
Those feeble handfuls back to English shores.

CHARLES

Then charge again. If heaven is with us,   30
We cannot lose the day.

KING JOHN

On, away!

Exit

ACT 4 ◆ SCENE 8

Enter Audley wounded and rescued by two squires

ESQUIRE

All well, my lord?

AUDLEY

As well as any man may be
That dines at such a bloody feast as this.

ESQUIRE

I hope, my lord, that is no mortal gash.

AUDLEY

No matter if it is; the score is cast   5
And means, at worst, the loss of one man's life.
Good friends, convey me to the princely Edward,
That in the bloody crimson of my dress
I may impress him with my lineaments.

I'll smile and tell him that this open scar   10
Completes the harvest of Lord Audley's war.

Exit

ACT 4 ◆ SCENE 9

Enter Prince Edward, King John, Charles, and all with ensigns
spread. Retreat sounded.

PRINCE EDWARD

Now, John of Valois, erstwhile John of France,
Your bloody standards are my captive colors;
And you, high-handed Charles of Normandy,
That sent me earlier a horse to flee,
Are now the subjects of my clemency.   5
Come, lords, is it not a shame that English boys,
Who have not even earned their beards yet
Outnumbered too, should rout you all at once
Within the bosom of your kingdom thus?

KING JOHN

Good fortune, not your force, defeated us.   10

PRINCE EDWARD

Ay, proof that heaven helps the righteous side.

Sound trumpets. Enter Artois and Philip.

O, look, Artois! And by his side he brings along
The pious counsel-giver to my soul.
Welcome, Artois, and welcome, Philip, too.
Which of us, do you think, now needs to pray?   15
I see the proverb manifest in you:
Too bright a morning brings a dismal day.

Enter Audley with Squires

But wait, what pallid aspect is this here?
Alas, what thousand armed men of France
Have marked this note of death in Audley's face?   20

Speak, you that woos death with a careless smile,
And looks so merrily upon your grave
As if you were enamored with your death.
What hungry sword has so bereaved your face
And cleaved a true friend from my loving soul?   25
AUDLEY
  O Prince, your kind and mournful speech to me
  Tolls like a deathknell to a sickly man.
PRINCE EDWARD
  If I too rashly rang out your demise,
  My arms will be your grave. What can I do
  To repair your life or to avenge your death?   30
  If honor may annul this death for you,
  Take all the everlasting honor here
  On this triumphant day, Audley, and live!
AUDLEY
  Victorious prince — and that is what you are —
  Behold the kings in your captivity —   35
  If I could stall dim death just for a bit
  Till I could see my liege your royal father,
  My soul would quit this castle of my flesh,
  This mangled tribute, freely of my will,
  To darkness, consummation, dust, and worms.   40
PRINCE EDWARD
  Luckily, brave mentor, your soul's too proud
  To yield her castle with a single breach.
  Here, to redress your life I give to you
  Three thousand marks a year in English land.
AUDLEY
  I take your gift to pay the debts I owe.   45
  These two poor squires have saved me from the French
  With dire and utmost hazard of their lives.

What you have given me, I offer them;
And, if you love me, Prince, lay your consent
To this bequest in my last testament. 50

PRINCE EDWARD

O honored Audley, live, and have from me
This gift twice doubled to these squires and you.
But live or die, what you have sacrificed
For us ensures that sovereignty abides.
Come, gentlemen, I will see my friend conveyed 55
To more commodious chambers. Then we'll march
Proudly toward Calais with triumphant pace
To pay my royal father tribute due
For these my wars with France's king and son.

Exit

ACT 5 ◆ SCENE 1

Enter six citizens in their shirts, barefoot, with nooses about their
necks. Enter King Edward, Queen Philippa, Derby, and soldiers.

KING EDWARD

No more, Queen Philippa, be you assured,
Copeland, unless he can explain his lapse,
Will see displeasure plainly in our looks.
And now about this proud, resistant town.
Soldiers, assault! I will no longer wait   5
To be deluded by their sham delays.
Put all to death, and plunder as you please.

CITIZENS

Mercy, King Edward, mercy, gracious lord.

KING EDWARD

Contemptible villains, now you call for truce?
My ears are deaf against your futile cries.   10
Drum the call to arms; draw your killing swords!

CITIZEN ONE

Ah, noble lord, take pity on this town,
And hear us, mighty King.
We serve the promise that your highness made:
The two days' deadline is not yet expired,   15
And we are come to willingly endure
What torturing death or punishment you please,
So that the trembling multitude are spared.

KING EDWARD

My promise? Well, I do confess as much;
But I demanded leading citizens   20
And men of highest standing to enlist.

You, very likely, are lowly townsmen,
Or some arrested pirates from the sea,
Whom no doubt the law would execute,
Even if we chose to exercise our mercy.   25
No, no, you can't outwit us thus again.

CITIZEN TWO

The sun, dread Lord, that in the western rim
Beholds us now so miserably bereft,
Did in the eastern purple of the morn
Salute us once as gentry of Calais.   30
All true, or may our lot be with the damned.

KING EDWARD

If this is so, then let our covenant stand:
We take possession of the town in peace.
As for yourselves, there will be no remorse
But, as imperial justice so decrees,   35
Your bodies shall be dragged around these walls,
And after, feel the stroke of severing steel.
This is your doom. Go, soldiers, see it done.

QUEEN PHILIPPA

Ah, show some lenience to these yielding men.
It is a glorious thing to foster peace   40
And gracious kings themselves are most like God
When giving life and life's largess to all.
If your intent is to be king of France
Then let her people live to call you king,
For whom the sword cuts down or fire chars   45
Pays no due homage to the champion.

KING EDWARD

Although the past has taught us this is true,
That peaceful transition is most preferred
When occupation's crimes are most restrained,

Yet, insofar as we are obliged to prove   50
That we can master our passions as well
As we can master men by rule of sword,
My queen prevails: we yield to your request.
These men are saved by your wise clemency
And Tyranny has no confederates.   55

CITIZEN TWO

Long live your highness! Happy be your reign!

KING EDWARD

Go, all of you, return home to your town;
And if this kindness has earned half your love,
Then learn to cherish Edward as your king.

Exit citizens

Now let us deal with our affairs abroad.   60
We might, till gloomy winter passes on,
Repost our men in garrison awhile.

Enter Copeland with King David

DERBY

Copeland, my lord, with David, King of Scots.

KING EDWARD

Is this the proud presuming squire of the north
That would not yield his prisoner to my Queen?   65

COPELAND

I am, my liege, a northern squire indeed,
But neither proud nor insolent, I hope.

KING EDWARD

What moved you, then, to be immovably
Set against our royal Queen's desire?

COPELAND

No willful disobedience, mighty lord,   70
Just doing as the code of war prescribes.
I fought the king and took him one-on-one,

.

85

And, like a soldier, would be loath to lose
The least distinction that this has won me.
So Copeland, which I am, to your majesty   75
Now comes to France, and with a lowly bow
Does sweetly tip his top in victory.
Receive, dread lord, the tribute of my freight,
The pricey prince of my laboring hands,
Which I would surely have surrendered up,   80
Had but your grace been there to take the man.

QUEEN PHILIPPA

But, Copeland, you ignored the King's command,
Defying our commission in his name.

COPELAND

His name I honor, but his person more.
I'll always swear allegiance to his name,   85
But to his person I will bend my knee.

KING EDWARD

I urge you, Phillipa, let your umbrage pass.
This man amuses me, and I like his words;
For who among us would attempt great deeds
And spurn the glory that proceeds from them?   90
All rivers have recourse back to the sea,
As Copeland's faith courses back to his king.
Kneel, esquire, down: now rise, King Edward's knight;
And, to maintain your lands, I allocate
Five hundred marks a year to you and yours.   95

Enter Salisbury

Welcome, Lord Salisbury. What news from Brittany?

SALISBURY

This, mighty King: the country now is ours,
And Charles de Mountford, regent of that place,
Presents your highness with this coronet,

Proclaiming true allegiance to your grace.   100
KING EDWARD
    We thank you for your service, valiant earl:
    Dote on our favor, for we owe you that.
SALISBURY
    But now, my lord, as this was joyful news,
    I must adjust my voice to tragical,
    And sing of most despondent spectacles.   105
KING EDWARD
    What, have our men been overthrown at Poitiers,
    And is our son beset with murderous odds?
SALISBURY
    He was, my lord; I traveled there myself
    With forty of my most intrepid knights,
    Under safe-conduct of the dauphin's seal   110
    To join the prince. But then to our distress,
    A troop of lancers met us on the way,
    Arrested us and brought us to the king,
    Who using this to mete out some revenge,
    Commanded at once to cut off our heads;   115
    And surely we'd have died, but that the duke,
    More bound by honor than his father was,
    Procured our quick deliverance from there.
    But, as we went, "Salute your king," said he.
    "Bid him prepare a funeral for his son.   120
    Today our sword will cut his thread of life
    And sooner than he thinks we'll be with him
    To redress those injuries he has done."
    This said, we left, not daring to reply.
    Our hearts were dead, our looks diffuse and gaunt.   125
    Wandering, at last we climbed atop a hill,
    From where, although our grief was hard before,

Yet now, to see this moment with our eyes
Did three times more increase our heaviness.
For there, my lord, oh, there we did discern   130
Down in a valley how both armies lay:
The French had dug their trenches like a ring,
And every barricade's wide open front
Was thick embossed with rude artillery.
Here, a cavalry of ten thousand horse;   135
There, twice as many pikes in squares arranged;
Here crossbows and deadly piercing spears;
And in the center, like a distant point
Stood your son Edward, waiting for the hour
Those dogs of France would rush him and his men.   140
In time the death-declaring bell begins:
Off go the cannons, that with rumbling noise
Convulsed the very mountain where they stood.
Then sound the trumpets' clangor in the air;
The armies clash and, when we could no more   145
Determine who was friend and who the foe
So tangled up the dark confusion was,
We turned away our wat'ry eyes, our sighs
As black as powder fuming into smoke.
And thus, I fear, I may have sadly told   150
The most untimely tale of Edward's fall.

QUEEN PHILIPPA

Ah me, is this my welcome into France?
Is this the comfort that I looked to have
When I prepared to meet my beloved son?
Sweet Ned, I gladly would have drowned at sea   155
To keep this mortal grief from killing me.

KING EDWARD

There, Phillipa, content, no tears will serve

To call him back if he's been taken there.
Console yourself as I do, gentle queen,
With hopes of some unthought-of dire revenge.   160
He asked me to arrange a funeral for him
And so I will, but all the peers of France
Shall mourners be and weep forth tears of blood
Until their empty veins are dry and raw.
The pillars of his hearse shall be their bones;   165
The clay that covers him, their cities' ashes;
His requiem the cries of dying men;
And in the place of tapers on his tomb
A hundred fifty towers shall blaze in France
While we lament our valiant Edward's death.   170

After a flourish sounded within, enter a Herald

HERALD

Rejoice, my lord! Ascend the imperial throne!
The mighty and remorseless Prince of Wales,
Great kinsman to the God of War himself,
The scourge of Frenchmen and Toast of England,
Triumphant, rides in like a Roman lord,   175
And stumbling at his lowly stirrup's side
King John of France with his son Philip comes
In captive bonds; whose ring of gold he brings
To crown you with, and so proclaim you king.

KING EDWARD

Away with mourning, Philippa, wipe your eyes!   180
Sound, trumpets, welcome in Plantagenet!

Enter Prince Edward, King John, Philip, Audley, and Artois

As long lost trinkets are treasures when found
So does my son convert my heart to gold
Which even now was cracked and crumbling stone.

QUEEN PHILIPPA

    Accept this token to express my joy —   185

(she kisses him)

    For inward passions will not let me speak.

PRINCE EDWARD

    My gracious father, here receive the gift,

    This wreath of conquest and reward of war,

    Seized with as stout a peril to our lives

    As any hallowed object ever was.   190

    Assume your proper right to wear this crown

    And herewith do I render to your hands

    These prisoners, chief conductors of our strife.

KING EDWARD

    So, John of France, I see you keep your word:

    You promised to be sooner in our midst   195

    Than we supposed, and here you are indeed.

    But had you done at first what now you do,

    How many cities might have stood untouched

    That now are razed to jagged heaps of stones.

    How many people's lives might you have saved   200

    That have untimely sunk into their graves.

KING JOHN

    Edward, why speak of things irrevocable?

    Tell me what ransom will pay my release.

KING EDWARD

    Your ransom, John, will soon enough be known.

    But first to England you must cross the seas,   205

    To see what entertainment waits for you.

    Whatever happens cannot be as bad

    As the diversions we endured in France.

KING JOHN

    Accursèd man! Of this I was foretold,

But misconstrued the words the prophet told. 210

PRINCE EDWARD

Now, father, I as prince request one thing
Of you, whose grace has been my strongest shield:
That, as your prudence chose me for the man
To show the world your right ascendant power,
So should those other princely warriors 215
Bred and burnished up within that little isle
Achieve their own success in serving you.
And as for me, the bloody scars I bear,
And weary nights that I stood watch alone,
The dangerous conflicts that were slung at me, 220
The fearful menaces that came my way,
The heat and cold and torments in-between,
I wish were now redoubled twenty times,
So that in future days, when they do read
The painful traffic of my tender youth, 225
These princes' resolve might be so inflamed,
That not only France's provinces,
But also any country on this earth
That would unjustly stoke fair England's ire,
Will at their presence tremble and retire. 230

KING EDWARD

Here, English lords, we do proclaim a rest,
An intermission to our costly wars.
Sheathe up your swords, refresh your weary limbs,
Inspect your spoils; and after we have breathed
A day or two within this haven town, 235
God willing then for England we set sail,
Where, on a better day, I trust, we shall
Arrive three kings, two princes, and a queen.

Exit